"MAN'S BEST FRIEND"

(But The Entire City Loves Him)

By

JOHN A. GREER SR.

(New Author)

President and CEO of Baskart International Incorporated, Poe Pemp's Incorporated, Allen's International Incorporated (A.I.) and Marvenus Multi-purpose Mammoth S.A.F.E Center. 325 Hwy 80 E. Suite 106 Clinton, Ms 39056

Future Author of
Books that will help inspire all ages to believe that they can achieve.

ALOFUS

Man's Best Friend

"But the Entire City Loves Him"

This is the story of a city that fell in love with a Bionic Dog
Named Alofus
Synonymous to All of Us

JOHN A. GREER SR.

Order this book online at www.trafford.com
or email orders@trafford.com

Most Trafford titles are also available at major online book retailers.

Printed in the United States of America.

ISBN: 978-1-4269-5408-5 (sc)
ISBN: 978-1-4269-5409-2 (hc)
ISBN: 978-1-4269-5410-8 (e)

Library of Congress Control Number: 2011900176

Trafford rev. 01/18/2011

 www.trafford.com

North America & International
toll-free: 1 888 232 4444 (USA & Canada)
phone: 250 383 6864 ♦ fax: 812 355 4082

What This Story "Man's Best friend, But The Entire City Loves Him" is all about.

To begin, this story is fictional and is primarily about a dog, but as it progresses, it becomes somewhat of a soap opera, stemming from the supporting cast surrounding the main character, Alofus (the dog). Alofus' family falls in love with him, as does the entire city. Alofus is introduced in the story as the lone survivor of a litter of puppies. Though this Australian sheperd initially belonged to NaNa and Paw Paw, it will ultimately be owned by their grandson (Little Jay), who is another featured star in the story. Little Jay is a 10 year old Afro-American boy living in Jackson, Mississippi along with his mom, dad, and sister. Little Jay's sister is named Diamerald Alexus. She is a 17 year old senior in high school and is about to graduate. Little Jay's mom is currently a home maker, but is about to embark upon a new venture in life and become a pharmacist at a local drug store. And Little Jay's dad is presently a sergeant on the police force, there in Jackson, Mississippi, who is about to be promoted to lieutenant as overseer of the homicide division.

The
Things that an individual will learn from reading this book, though it
is fictional, is that
if we work together for the common good of humanity and
Man's Best Friend,
we can defeat anything that might get in the way.

What this book will attempt to prove is that when an individual
(or an Entire City) has love and perseverance, they have hope and
strength.

This book is dedicated to
Everyone who has Man's Best Friend
As a companion,
People who love Dogs
And moreover, humankind as we now know it.

CRITIQUE
This thrill-filled novel has an eloquent nature, and is so
entertaining, that the entire family will enjoy it...
Because of Alofus' and the other main characters' likeable
personalities,
the readers will find themselves falling in love with this book, thus
making it somewhat of a love story...

Reading comprised of
D-SCARF
Drama--that is delineative and realistic,
Suspense--that will keep you guessing and on your toes,
Comedy--that is sporadic,
Action--that readers will anticipate seeing on the big screen,
Romance--that is unadulterated, and
Friendship- that exemplifies loyalty and unity among the family
(Stay tuned for future books to come with the D-SCARF syndrome
in mind.)

"Man's Best Friend"
(But the Entire City Loves Him)
<u>Alofus</u>-synonymous to (All of Us)

    ***In this story, a city plagued by schism, violence, and despodency unites to help a father, a son, and his dog,
        who are the only ones brave enough to step forward and fight, to save the hopeless city,
        which is being ruined by a couple of villains, who you will come to know within this story.***

Created by
John A. Greer Sr.

Cast of Characters in the Story

1. Alofus: Little Jay's dog
2. Little Jay. Jonathan Dooley, Jr.
3. Mr. Dooley. Jonathan Dooley, Sr- A Policeman.
4. NaNa: Little Jay's grandma
5. Paw Paw: Little Jay's grandpa
6. Missy: NaNa and Paw Paw's dog
7. Mrs. Dooley: Lillian Dooley
8. Diamerald Alexus: Little Jay's sister
9. Jimmy: June Bug- Bully #1
10. Robi: Bully #2.
11. Mr. Giradeli: Robi's dad
12. Ms. Nuttingham: Jimmy's grandma
13. Nappy Headed Squirrel: Kenny (young man) - Associate of June Bug
14. Guy at Counter: Works at the pool hall
15. Manager: Manages the pool hall
16. Guy in Vehicle: Informant who flags Mr. Dooley down ouside of the pool hall
17. Money Mike: Alfred Kincade- Mr. Dooley's nemesis
18. Serg. Willansby: Friend and ex girlfriend of Mr. Dooley
19. Dr. Elenski: Former professor at the university- Creator of M&M's Pool Hall
20. Dr. Satcher: Former president of the college board
21. Dr. Olgaston: Director of personnel at JSU
22. Professor Greer : Present director over the lab- Former co worker and assistant of Dr. Elenski
23. Hanna: Diamerald's room mate
24. Chief McClemens: Chief of Police Dept.
25. Barbara: Serg. Willansby's daughter
26. Kellie: Mrs. Dooley's sister
27. Mark: Kellie's son
28. Officer Bradley: Ofc. That calls Mr. Dooley about Alofus
29. Officer Lansing: Ofc. who found Alofus injured.
30. Corporal Davenport: Ofc.ordered to move crowd back at crime scene

WHY I WROTE THIS BOOK

I have yet to meet a human being that has the best of every physical attribute- beauty, brawn, and brilliance. Whenever we strive to have something a certain way, better than it already is, we are by definition, fighting a losing battle. Rather than being thankful and content with the card life dealt us, we as a people, focus on what's wrong with our bodies and our need to change it. Sad yet true, zeroing in on our defects implies that we are dissatisfied with ourselves... For what?... Carrying a few extra, undesirable pounds? Not running as fast as some other people? Not being as strong as some other people? Looking older than people who are actually older than us? The very act of focusing on these imperfections distracts us from the real reason God created us, which is to love one another, no matter the features. Don't get me wrong, the body is God's temple and he wants us to maintain it. However, even though there's always room for improvement, we should be careful not to become obsessed by putting too much emphasis on our looks. Remember... everything God created was good... very good. Therefore, we should enjoy and appreciate who we are. And besides, as we have borne the image of the earthy, we shall also bear the image of the heavenly. For this corruptible must put on incorruption, and this mortal must put on immortality. In a world where judgment is absent, every**body** is good. So in closing, this is why I decided to create such a book, to help enlighten the readers about the dangers of tampering with God's creations... mankind and man's best friend.

Acknowledgments

I would like to acknowledge the following for inspiring and assisting me in the creation of this book. First and foremost, I thank God almighty and His son, Jesus Christ, for waking me up in the middle of the night and impressing upon my mind of heart to write such a story. It was meant to be a fictive narrative. However, it does, somewhat, sing of my own personal life, thus creating (I guess you could say) a half truth narrative.

I'd also like to thank my mom, Mary Greer Watson, who was called home to glory on February 20, 2008. And to my uncle Wilce (Buddy) Day, who also passed away in 2009. To the both of them who afforded me with the attributes to be the man that I have become. I'll always love you both mom, Uncle Buddy and I will see you all on the other side. And to my lovely and beautiful wife, Valerie Janet, the fruit of her own works praise her, in that our children rose up and called her blessed. She has been good to me all "The days of our lives together" (29) wonderful years. In so much that her value truly outweighs the price of rubies. Thank you, Lord Jesus, for such a wonderful help mate. Also there is another interesting individual in my life that I couldn't dare not make mention,. my dear aunt and second mom, Pearline Johnson. For by her awesome and unchanging faith, she inspires me to continue to trust in the Lord. I'll never forget her. And to Dee, thanks for her enthusiasm and encouragement surrounding this book. I'd like to also say thanks to my darling children; Tracy, Jacelyn, John Jr. (BKA) D.J. Slim., Shawn, Arionne, Jeffrey, and Alexis, as well as my grandchildren; Destiny, Trerell, Lazaria, Johanah, Janeece, and Latrell. I'd like to thank my adopted children; Zanetta, Sparklette, Diamond, Jeffrey, and Jeremy for their insightful inputs. I want to give a special thanks to Sparklette for her visionistic and humble spirit, which helped me to put this book together, and to my second eldest son, Shawn, for his inspiring editorial skills and his equal love for the Lord. And last but not least, thanks to a couple of brothers of mine, Melvin, and Archie. Also I would like to mention two other dear friends, Robert and Shirley Marion for their kind support. For without God's guidance and His Devine inspiration and from everyone that was involved, I could not have done it. Thank you all very much for helping me to bring this book into fruition.

John A. Greer Sr.

"Man's Best Friend"
(But the Entire City Loves Him)
Alofus-synonymous to All of Us

Created By
John A. Greer Sr.

To explain how Alofus came about and was acquainted with the Dooley family, a while back, the Dooleys got a visit from NaNa and Paw Paw, Little Jay's and Diamerald Alexus' grandparents. NaNa and Paw Paw had a dog named Missy, who was a female Australian shepherd and was pregnant. Missy went into labor prematurely and gave birth to six puppies. Unfortunately, due to medical complications, five of the six puppies died within twenty four hours. So NaNa and

Paw Paw were determined to save the last puppy. They took it to the vet and it was put on life support in an incubator. Consequentially, NaNa and Paw Paw got lots of support from all over the city. The puppy gained lots of popularity and fame for his determination to live. Everyone prayed for the puppy and donated money to help with the expenses of saving it. After about six weeks passed, the doctor of the veterinarian hospital gave a thumbs up that the puppy was okay, and that it could survive on its own. Everyone in the city was thrilled, aside from a few individuals who found it absurd for the city to put so much emphasis on an animal. Nevertheless, NaNa and Paw Paw never lost faith. Missy was also thrilled that one of her puppies survived. She showed it by almost licking him to death as the cameras from the media captured that special moment. Almost two months passed and NaNa and Paw Paw had gotten so caught up in trying to save Missy's lone puppy that they had almost forgotten about their grandson, Little Jay, whose birthday was on the very next day. So NaNa, Paw Paw, and Missy got in their car and rode across town to take the surviving puppy to him for his birthday, because he always used to say, when Missy had her puppies, he would surely want one, and that he wanted to go hunting with his dad, Paw Paw, and the dog after it had fully grown. When it was time for NaNa, Paw Paw and Missy to return home, it was getting late and had begun to rain. So they all got into the car and headed home. Unfortunately, they didn't make it back home. They were all killed in a car wreck when Paw Paw lost control of the vehicle and went over an embankment due to a strange obstacle running in front of the car... So now, here we are; at the Dooleys' residence on the day of the funeral. After the funeral, the Dooley family lounges in the family room and dad begins to speak...

Mr. Dooley: Now I know that all of us are still grieving over the loss of NaNa, Paw Paw, and Missy but we do have something to help us remember all of them by: the puppy that they gave Little Jay as a gift. So why don't you name your new friend?

Little Jay: Dad... mom... Diamerald Alexus... I just wanna say that, yeah, I miss NaNa, Paw Paw, and Missy and, of course, I love the new puppy that I got for my birthday. I always wanted a dog, and had hopes of going hunting with it and Paw Paw and dad one day, but all that has changed now that NaNa, Paw Paw, and Missy are dead. I thought it would be hard for me to think of a name for the puppy, but it wasn't. As a matter of fact, I dreamt of a name for it just last night, and that name is All of Us.

(Little Jay pauses and drops his head, gloomily)

Diamerald Alexus: Little Jay?... All of us what?... All of what, Little Jay?

Mrs. Dooley: (Walks over to Little Jay and puts her arms around him) Are you okay, sweetie?

Mr. Dooley: Son, it's okay, tell us what you want all of us to do.

Little Jay: Nothing, I'm not asking you all to do anything... I mean, yeah, I'm hurting and sad about losing NaNa, Paw Paw and Missy but I am well enough to to tell you all what we should name the puppy; and that's what I am doing. Let's name him All of Us.

Diamerald Alexus: Mom... dad... I know that we just lost NaNa, Paw Paw and Missy and all, but Little Jay is trippin', talking about naming a dog
All of Us; that's stupid.

Mrs. Dooley· (In Little Jay's defense) Diamerald, you ought to be ashamed of yourself, talking ill of your little brother like that, especially at a time like this.

Mr. Dooley: Yeah, Diamerald, this is not the time for you to be challenging your brother's intellect. I want you to apologize to him this instant.

Diamerald Alexus: Oh, alright mom and dad! (Turns to Little Jay) Little Jay, I'm sorry. Mom and dad are right, I shouldn't have said those things to you about that name for your puppy. Afterall, he is your puppy... Do you forgive me, Little Jay?

Little Jay: Of course I forgive you, Diamerald, and thanks for your apology but you didn't have to apologize. I know why you said what you did, and if it wasn't for my dream last night, I probably would've been agreeing with you. I thought it was a message from God, the fact that this idea came to me in a dream just last night. And since all of us are sad about the losing NaNa, Paw Paw and Missy, then the puppy automatically became special to All of Us; that's all. (He drops his head again.)

Mr. Dooley: Son, I am very proud of you and how you handled your sister's remarks, without lashing back at her in a negative way. Also, after hearing you explain your reason for giving the puppy that name in such a mature way, while considering our feelings, I think that it would truly be an honor for the puppy to bear that name.

Mrs. Dooley: (Hugs Little Jay) You see, Little Jay? Haven't I always told you how bright you were? I love you, son.

Diamerald Alexus: (Walks over and kisses Little Jay on the cheek) I'm glad to have you as a brother, Little Jay, and I do love that name (All of Us). But can I interject one thing in regards to the spelling of the name? Can we leave off one letter (L) so that it would be pronounced A-Lo'Fus (OL'iv'us), like as in outlive us? Because I truly hope that you and the puppy out live all of us, Little Jay. Both of you are very special to us and I don't know how I would get along without you two.

Mrs. Dooley: Ah, honey, that was such a sweet thing to say to your little brother. But you're something special to us too, baby girl, and we love you just as much.

Mr. Dooley: Yeah, sweetheart, that sounds wonderful to me, (Little Jay nods his head) and I see that your brother is also in agreement with your suggestions. This incident just goes to show that you two knuckle heads can work together for one common good (being sarcastic).

(Everyone in the room laughs at this remark)

Little Jay: Then it's official, mom... dad... Diamerald... we all agree to call him Alofus?
(Simultaneously, Mr. Dooley, Mrs. Dooley, and Diamerald reply, "Yes, we do." Then Diamerald walks over to Little Jay and hugs him, and they both begin to jump up and down, chanting "Alofus! Alofus!")

**Stay tuned for the conclusion:
"You don't want to miss it"**

"Man's Best Friend"
(But the Entire City Loves Him)
Continuation-(1 year later)

By John A. Greer Sr.

Now here we are, 12 months after the Dooley family discussed the puppy's name. In addition to Alofus now being fully grown, the family has had some alterations of its own. Little Jay, who is now 11 years old, has also grown a couple of inches taller and has transitioned from grade school to middle school. His sister Diamerald Alexus, who is now 18 years old, has graduated from senior high and is enrolled at Jackson State, a major university where she is a science major. Mrs. Dooley is no longer a homemaker, but is employed with a local pharmaceutical firm. And Mr. Dooley, who is a police officer, has been promoted from sergeant to lieutenant. On top of all that, the Dooley family has just moved into their new home, which is located in a more upscale neighborhood. Little Jay is having problems adapting to both his new school and his new neighborhood. Being that his dad is a cop, a couple of the guys in the neighborhood and at school have been bullying Little Jay because their dads have had problems with cops in the past and have shared stories about the incidents with them. Now Little Jay is enduring the aftermath of the ordeals, and has started conveying to his dad that he would rather him not be a cop. He implies that he would like his dad to quit being a cop because of the possibilities of him getting killed. But his dad finds this to be a little odd since he is now assigned to more desk duty, whereas when he was a sergeant, he had more street patrol, yet Little Jay didn't complain at all then. So Mr. Dooley is determined to find out the real reason Little Jay is campaigning for him to change his profession, and that is where we come in on the conclusion of this story.

(As Mr. Dooley drives his squad car into his driveway, he notices Little Jay out in front of his home with a couple of his friends... or at least that's what they appear to be...)

Mr. Dooley: (Gets out of the car) Hey, son. What's going on? Is everything all right?

(Little Jay has a hesitant look on his face, because he's really in the company of the two bullies.)

Little Jay: Yeah, dad, everything's okay. 'Just hanging out with my friends.

Two Bulies: Good evening, Mr. Dooley. How are you?

Mr. Dooley: I'm okay; thanks for asking. Are you guys staying out of trouble?

(All three boys respond simultaneously...)

Little Jay: Yeah, dad   Two Bullies: Yes sir, Mr. Dooley.

Mr. Dooley: Okay, then keep up the good work. Now, Little Jay, you come in shortly so you can get prepared to eat supper.

Little Jay: Ah-ite dad, I will.

(When Mr. Dooley goes into the house, the two bullies immediately walk over to Little Jay.)

Bully #2: How come your dad always talks about staying out of trouble, as if everybody's subject to do something bad?

Little Jay: I don't know, it bugs me, too. But I told ya'll I was trying to get my dad to quit being a cop. Just give me a little more time, and my dad will change jobs; you'll see.

(Both bullies laugh...)

Two Bullies: Yeah right; keep dreaming, Little Jay.

Little Jay: Okay guys; that's not fair. Anyway, I'm about to go inside. I'll see you all at school tomorrow.

Bully #1: Yeah, you do that. And you better not forget to bring our lunch money, or else...

(Little Jay stares fearfully and walks into his house.)

(Now Mr. Dooley, Mrs. Dooley, and Little Jay are gathered at the dinner table, prepared to eat...)

Mr. Dooley: Son, do you want to do the honors and lead the grace?

Little Jay: Ah, dad, I don't know how to say grace. Besides, God doesn't listen to me anyway.

Mrs. Dooley: Little Jay, what are you saying? Just where on earth did you get such a ridiculous notion?

Mr. Dooley: Son, I know that we are about to eat supper, but is there something bothering you? Because if there is, you know that we are here for you. I just want you to know that God does listen to kids. Even in the Bible, it says "Suffer the little children to come unto me and forbid them not; for such is the kingdom of God".

Mrs. Dooley: Yeah, Little Jay. We want you to feel like you can always come to us for anything. Now tell mommy and daddy, what's really bothering our little guy?

Little Jay: (is stunned that his parents know that his problem is not really about God listening to him) Well mom and dad, to tell you all the truth, I know that God does listen to me and I want to apologize for such an unfair statement because a year ago, before I went to bed, I asked God to help me with a name for my new puppy and I ended up with an answer from Him in a dream... and that worked out perfectly.

Mr. Dooley: Yes, it certainly did, son. So now are you ready to tell us what possessed you to make such an outrageous statement?

Mrs. Dooley: Little Jay, is it that you are still upset about Diamerald Alexus choosing to live on campus? I know how hurt you were when your sister left home.

Little Jay: No mom, it has nothing to do with Diamerald Alexus, but it does have something to do with dad.

Mr. Dooley: Me? What does God not listening to you have to do with me, son?

Little Jay: (Mr. and Mrs. Dooley eagerly await his answer)

Well, dad, I've been praying for you to give up your job as a policeman and do something different, and for six months now nothing has changed.

Mrs. Dooley: Son, why would you want your dad to give up his job, something that he loves and that helps to pay the bills so that we can eat and enjoy all the other things we need money for?

Mr. Dooley: Little Jay, if you can honestly tell me why you want me to give up my job as a policeman, then I will seriously consider retiring from the force.

Little Jay: Really?! Do you mean it, dad?! You'd do that for me?!

Mr. Dooley: Yeah son, I would, but first you must confess to me and your mom... I noticed that you said you'd been asking God of this matter for six months now: that's about how long we've been in our new home here. Now that wouldn't have anything to do with this matter, would it?

Little Jay: Okay, dad... mom... since I promised to come clean if dad considered retiring... well, moving into this new home was great and all, but it has caused me to have to go to a new school and make new friends. However, that hasn't carried over too well for me.

Mr. Dooley: How is that, son? Didn't I just see you outside with two of your new friends?

Little Jay: Well, I guess, but they're not as cool as my old friends back at my old school and neighborhood.

Mrs. Dooley: Not cool?... What do you mean not cool? You never told us about any of your friends being cool, Little Jay. So what's really going on here?

Mr. Dooley: I think I know what's wrong with Little Jay, honey... Those uncool friends of his are probably badgering him about me being a cop.

(Little Jay drops his head with no response)

Mrs. Dooley: Little Jay, is that the case, son? Is there anybody threatening you?

Little Jay: Ah, alright mom and dad... I hate it when you all are able to detect when something is wrong with me.

Mr. Dooley: That's our job as parents, son. And aren't you glad that I am a cop who's smart enough to help solve some of the problems we have in our society? Although that's a big task, and it's not much, it's a start on making our city and the world a little safer.

Little Jay: (yells with tears in his eyes) Yeah right! Well what about me, dad? Why isn't it safe for me to go outside or to school, huh? If it's such a good thing for you to be a cop, how come they pick on me so much?

Mrs. Dooley: (gets up and walks over to Little Jay to comfort him) Little Jay, what's with all this, son? What's really going on with you?

Mr. Dooley: I know what's going on... some of the same stuff Diamerald Alexus experienced when she was younger. Little Jay is being brain washed and bullied.

Mrs. Dooley: Is that true, Little Jay? Is anyone talking ill to you about your dad being a cop, or threatening you in any kind of way?

Little Jay: (hangs his head as if mom hit a weak spot) Well mom... dad... to be honest, I have been having to deal with some things that Jimmy and Robi's been dishing out.

Mr. Dooley: Who is Jimmy and Robi, son?

Mrs. Dooley: Honey, that's the two young men who were outside with Litttle Jay when you drove up, just a minute ago.

Mr. Dooley: Are you serious? They seem like such good boys, very well mannered.

Little Jay: Yeah dad, that's what I thought, they fooled me too. But to be honest, they have been bashing your job and bullying me ever since we got here, and I didn't want to tell you all because I thought I could handle it myself.

Mrs. Dooley: Son, don't ever feel like you need to handle something like this by yourself. This is serious business, and you need an adult's input. Okay?

Little Jay: Alright, mom. I know that you all are right, and I'm sorry for not sharing this with you all sooner.

Mr. Dooley: It's okay, son. I'm just glad we got hold of this information before it got out of hand. Now let's see... how do you think we should handle this?

Little Jay: Actually, dad, I've run out of ideas so I'm leaving this up to you and mom, if that's okay.

Mrs. Dooley: Little Jay, I'm glad this got out in the open, and your dad and I will put a stop to this, don't you worry.

Little Jay: Uh-oh... What does that mean, mom? Will I still be able to show my face around here and at school?

Mr. Dooley: Sure you will, son... Everything's gonna be just fine.

Little Jay: Okay, dad, thanks. Now can I be excused? After all this commotion, I've lost my appetite.

Mrs. Dooley: Yeah, it's okay. I'll put your plate up just in case you want to eat later.
(Little Jay walks upstairs to his room)

Mr. Dooley: Do you think he's okay, honey? Should I go up there and speak with him?

Mrs. Dooley: No, not this time. Let's just do what we told him; let's make this thing go away... right now. The nerve of those boys! And to think, I've been feeding them lunch on Saturdays for a month now.

Mr. Dooley: (bangs his fist on the table in anger) I don't give a damn about the food or them questioning my profession, but no one bully's my son and gets away with it!

Mrs. Dooley: (walks over and puts her arms around Mr. Dooley) Settle down, honey. We will get through this, alright, and so will Little Jay, as did Diamerald Alexus.

Mr. Dooley: I know, honey, I'm sorry. By the way, where does Jimmy and Robi live? Have you met their parents at all?

Mrs. Dooley: Actually... no... To be honest, I don't even know where they live. I guess I blew this one, huh honey?

Mr.Dooley: Yeah, you did. You know the rules. Our kids don't collaborate with other kids when we don't know much about their backgrounds or their parents.

Mrs. Dooley: I know, honey, I'm sorry. I lost focus and it won't happen again.

Mr. Dooley: It's alright, sweetheart, we all slip at times. I'm going upstairs to see if Little Jay has any information on these two kids. (goes upstairs   and knocks on Little Jay's door)

Little Jay: Yes, who's there?

Mr. Dooley: It's dad; open up.

Little Jay: The door isn't locked. Come on in, dad.

Mr. Dooley: (twists the door knob and walks into Little Jay's room) Hey, son, how are you doing?

Little Jay: Oh, I'm okay, dad. What's up?

Mr. Dooley: Well, about our discussion downstairs... I'm going to get on it right away. How does that sound?

Little Jay: Sounds great to me. The sooner the better. Maybe then I could actually get some sleep at night.

Mr. Dooley: (smiles) Sure you will... absolutely. I'm sorry that you had to deal with an issue that was beyond your control, but don't you worry another minute, son. From here on out, dad's got your back.

Little Jay: I know that, dad. And again, I'm sorry for not coming forth with this sooner.

Mr. Doolcy: That's okay, son. The fact of the matter is that you did it before things got any worse. Now I'm gonna need one more favor from you.

Little Jay: What's that?

Mr. Dooley: I need you to tell me where Jimmy and Robi live.

Little Jay: Okay, dad, I will write down their addresses right now. (Little Jay writes down the addresses and hands it to Mr. Dooley.)

Mr. Dooley: (Reaches out and takes the paper) Thanks, son, I'll get back with you.

(Mr. Dooley walks out of the room, goes downstairs, and gets into his patrol car.)

(*A few minutes later, Mr. Dooley arrives at Robi's home. He gets out of the vehicle, walks to the door, and knocks. Then he hears a voice from the other side...*)

Voice: Who is it?

Mr. Dooley: Hello, this is Officer Dooley of the Jackson police department.

(The door opens, revealing a man with a puzzled look on his face, who seems to be wondering why a policeman is at his door...)

Man: Yes, can I help you, Officer?

Mr. Dooley: Well, sir, let me further introduce myself first.
(reaches out his hand to the man) How are you doing? I am Jonathan
Dooley.

Man: (shakes Mr. Dooley's hand) Okay, nice to meet you, Mr. Dooley.
I'm Mr. Giradeli. What can I do for you?

Mr. Dooley: Well... Mr. Giradeli, did you say?

Mr. Giradeli: Yes, that's correct.

Mr. Dooley: I have a son and his name is Jonathan, but we call him
Little Jay for short. You see, he's a junior. Anyhow, he and Robi
are friends, and I was just wondering if you were Robi's dad.

Mr. Giradeli: Yes, I am.

Mr. Dooley: Okay, good... Well, I don't really know how or where to
begin, but we will probably want to sit down on this one. May
I please come in?

Mr. Giradeli: Yeah sure, Mr. Dooley, come on in (steps aside and
invites Mr. Dooley to have a seat).

Mr. Dooley: Thanks (walks in and sits on the sofa).

Mr. Giradeli: (walks over to his recliner and sits) Okay, now what is it
and how can I help you? Robi hasn't gotten into any trouble,
has he?

Mr. Dooley: No, uh... no, not exactly. Is Robi here by any chance?

Mr. Giradeli: No, I'm sorry, he isn't. He and his mom went to the store
a moment ago to pick up a few items, but they should be back
shortly. What is it, Mr. Dooley? What's going on here? You got
my curiosity at its peak.

Mr. Dooley: Oh, alright... I can understand your position here, so I'll go ahead and inform you as to what's going on although, I must confess, I'd much rather have Robi and your wife present for this matter. However, since they are not present at the moment, I'll go ahead and discuss it with you for now.

Mr. Giradeli: Good, thank you (starts to get a bit agitated).

Mr. Dooley: Okay, then according to my son, Little Jay, Robi and his buddy, Jimmy, have been sort of bullying him around and badgering him about me being a cop. Now first, let me just say this, Mr. Giradeli... I'm not putting my son on a pedestal, and I'm not saying that he's an angel and doesn't get into mischief, but one thing that he doesn't do is lie to his parents; this I'm sure of. However, I'm only over here because there's always two sides to a story, and I'm hoping that Robi and Jimmy can shed some light on what's really going on. By the way- are you, by any chance, acquainted with Jimmy's parents?

Mr. Giradeli: Mr. Dooley, I do appreciate you coming over to discuss this matter with us about Robi, in such a dignified way... And if Robi has been indulging in such a cowardly act with Jimmy, then I promise we will get to the bottom of this matter and hopefully resolve it. Now, as for his friend, Jimmy... well, that's another issue, entirely. You see, my wife and I are not too fond of him ourselves.

Mr. Dooley: How come?

Mr. Giradeli: Well, Mr. Dooley... you see, just a few months ago, Robi and Jimmy had a spat with each other and, honestly, we didn't know that Robi and Jimmy were still collaborating with each other.

Mr. Dooley: Why not? What went on that caused such an issue?

Mr. Giradeli: What went on is that, Jimmy was at our house one evening after school, supposedly upstairs with Robi, working on a school project... However, what we found out is that they weren't working on a project at all. Instead, they were in Robi's room, smoking pot.

Mr. Dooley: (with amazement & dismay) Doing what?!

Mr. Giradeli: Hold on, Mr. Dooley, just wait til you hear the whole matter. Our Robi has never done anything like this before that day, or since then, to our knowledge... We found out that Jimmy is thirteen years old, two years older than our Robi. He has been in and out of juvenile detention ever since he was ten years old. His parents are not together. His mom left his dad... or so I heard... for another man, and his dad retaliated in anger and strangled her to death. He is now incarcerated, at the State Pen, for twenty years to life. And Jimmy is living with his grandma down the street, who hasn't been able to get a grip on the boy.

Mr. Dooley: That answers a lot of questions... Okay, thanks, Mr. Giradeli. I really appreciate you inviting me in and cooperating to help me get to the bottom of this. Can I leave my phone number with you? Maybe, one day, you and your family can join me and mine for dinner, so that we can all get better acquainted. After talking with you, I know that we won't be having any more problems with Robi, but if you have any further questions or need help with anything, please feel free to give me a call... anytime. Here's my card.

Mr. Giradeli: (takes the card) Thanks, Mr. Dooley... Oh, I see that you are a lieutenant on the force.

Mr. Dooley: Yes, just recently promoted.

Mr. Giradeli: Well, congratulations, and here is my card. Feel free to call me anytime as well.

Mr. Dooley: (takes the card) Oh, I see that you are vice president at the Regions Bank... Which branch?

Mr. Giradeli: The main office downtown... Drop in some time.

Mr. Dooley: I will. Actually, I've been meaning to change banks, anyhow. I haven't been too happy with the Trustmark Bank.

Mr. Giradeli: Good, you do that. We will be glad to have you all... and maybe I could get you on a good plan, (walks Mr. Dooley to the door)

Mr. Dooley: (leaving) Thanks and, again, nice meeting you Mr. Giradeli.

Mr. Giradeli: (closing the door) And thank you, Mr. Dooley. Good luck with your endeavor with Jimmy's grandma.

****[Mr. Dooley arrives at the home of Jimmy & his grandma, an old lady named Ms. Nuttingham, who is outside on the porch, winging in a love seat.]****

Mr. Dooley: (gets out of his car) Hello, how are you doing, ma'am?

Ms. Nuttingham: (is suspicious, but not amazed, that a policeman has shown up at her home) I'm okay, Offiza. Wutz June bug done did dis time?

Mr. Dooley: I'm sorry, ma'am, I don't know who you are referring to when you say June Bug.

Ms. Nuttingham: I'm talkin' bout my Litta Jimmy. Who is you? I thought all of you police offizas knowed Litta Jimmy.

Mr. Dooley: I'm Officer Dooley, ma'am, and I'm sorry... I don't know your Jimmy. You see, I was recently transferred to this district, so I don't know a lot of people in the area yet... but my son knows your Little Jimmy.

Ms. Nuttingham: Oh yeah? Who yo son is, mista?

Mr. Dooley: Little Jay. Do you know him? He and your grandson, Jimmy, have been hanging out at school together.

Ms. Nuttingham: Oh yeah, Litta Jay!... I know him, dat cute litta boy from 'round the corna. So dat's yo boy? He seems to be a good litta boy. Why he hangin' out wit Jimmy? Jimmy done gave up on life, so he ain't good company to nobody who wants somethin' outta life.

Mr. Dooley: I don't mean to be disrespectful to you, Ms. Nuttingham, but don't you think that's being a bit hard on your own grandson? Afterall, he is just a kid. Whatever is going on, there's still time to help Jimmy change and get on the right track.

Ms. Nuttingham: Litta Jimmy? Change? You might be ret, offiza, but I'ze been tryna help Jimmy fa three yearz now, n' it ain't done no good. So forgive my peckamittic attitude. I'ze done talked and talked, begged and begged... and I'm on my knees eva night, asking God to please touch Jimmy's heart and keep him safe. Sometimes I feel likes all hope is gone. Now I know dat ain't good thinking, and God is a good God, but
Ms. Nuttingham has gotten too ole and hu'a patience ain't likes it used to be. I need a ret now God... so iffin you gots some connections wit one, please sa, send him my way.

Mr. Dooley: Ms. Nuttingham! Now you know better than to be talking like that. We don't question or rush God. You know what they say, " He might not come when we want him to, but he's always on time".

Ms. Nuttingham: Well, he best be hurryin' up 'cause I ain't got much time left, n' neitha does Litta Jimmy at da rate he's going.

Mr. Dooley: I am so sorry to hear that you are having such a hard time with your grandson. I heard about how he lost both of his parents, and that's tragic... It must have had a big impact on Jimmy's rebellious behavior.

Ms. Nuttingham: Yeah, sho' it has, and dat's why I been fightin' fa him fa as long as I have, 'cause I'ze do loves him very much. But as I said earlia, Mr... uh... uh...

(Mr. Dooley helps her out with his name)

Mr. Dooley: Dooley. It's Mr. Dooley, ma'am.

Ms. Nuttingham: Yes, dat's it, Mista Dooley. Anyhow, as I was about to say, I'z tied... and I don't know how much longer I canz hold on fa Jimmy.

Mr. Dooley: I know, Ms. Nuttingham, but I'm glad I met you. I know now that it wasn't a mistake that we met. Perhaps, it's even God, finally answering your prayers.

Ms. Nuttingham: How so, Mista Dooley? What you mean by that?

Mr. Dooley: Well, Ms. Nuttingham, I initially came over to talk to you about your Little Jimmy... how he has been picking on my boy, Little Jay, and talking bad to him about me being a cop... but after hearing what you have said I know, without a shadow of a doubt, that God has other plans for this meeting.

Ms. Nuttingham: Wuchoo say? Plans? Wut in the world are you talkin' bout, mista?

Mr. Dooley: I'm talking about God working in mysterious ways. For my eyes have been opened and my heart has been enlightened to do something to help you save Little Jimmy... and I'm going to do just that.

Ms. Nuttingham: I don't know wut you talkin' bout, but iffin it means you gonna try and help my babi, then God bless yo soul.

Mr. Dooley: He already has, Ms. Nuttingham... He already has.

Ms. Nuttingham: Okay, I don't mean to be rude, mista but I'za got to be putting my suppa on... You mo' than welcome, though, to stay and have some.

Mr. Dooley: No ma'am, but thanks, anyway. I'll just be on my way... One other thing: Can you tell me where I can find Little Jimmy?

Ms. Nuttingham: Well, Jimmy ain't usually at no one pawticular place. He's a wandera, ya know? But you might have a chance of catching him at dat ole nappy headed squirrel's house just down yonder. He does spend lots of time wit dat feller.

Mr. Dooley: I'm sorry, I'm not understanding you. Did you say a nappy headed squirrel?

Ms. Nuttingham: Yeah, I said it! It's bad when a grown boy goes around wit his head lookin' lack they hasn't invented no combs yet. I'm talkin' bout dat there young man down the street, wit all the junk in his front yard and all e'm bad dogs... wut so never you call e'm.

Mr. Dooley: Are you talking about pit bull dogs, ma'am?

Ms. Nuttingham: Yeah, I think dat's wut Jimmy called e'm, spit full dogs. I heard dat they are called dat b'cause they always actin' crazi, lack they hates one anotha. Sometimes they get into a ruckus, ret he'a in front of my house.

Mr. Dooley: Okay, thanks, Ms. Nuttingham. I'll be in touch *(gets in the car and drives off)*

(Mr. Dooley drives slowly down the street, looking for a house that fits Ms. Nuttingham's description, with junk in the front yard and bad dogs.)

(He finally comes across such a house)
(He pulls up to the curve and looks around before exiting his vehicle, to ensure that he is safe from the bad dogs. As Mr. Dooley sits in his squad car, three huge, muscular, ferocious pit bulls run out from under the trash infested house to the fence surrounding it.. Then Mr. Dooley cautiously exits the vehicle, with his hand on his revolver, and commences to walk toward the house. As he does so, the dogs get even more irate and bark continually, while jumping up and down as if they are trying to hurdle the fence and get at Mr. Dooley, so Mr. Dooley stops in his tracks. Shortly thereafter, a young man, who fits Ms. Nuttingham's description of the nappy headed guy, comes out and commands the dogs to stop. All three dogs stop barking immediately and sit down like well trained animals. Then the young man yells out to Mr. Dooley...)

Young Man: What's up, Mr. Policeman? Who you looking for?

Mr. Dooley: First off, young man, if it's not asking too much, can you put your dogs away? Then I'll tell you what's up.

Young Man: Now why would I do that, Officer? Why I gotta put my dogs up when they are at home?

Mr. Dooley: Because if you don't, I am going to get on my two-way and call for animal control to come by your home and check the records, to see if your dogs are registered. Not only that... I will issue you a citation, myself, for violating the city leash law. Now beyond that, I think you already know how far this can go. So what up with you, Mr. Pit Bull Man?

Young Man: Okay partner, you da man, I didn't mean to get you all roused up or anything, ah-ite?

Mr. Dooley: Never mind all the chatter, guy, just do like I asked and everything will be ah-ite, partner.

(The young man whistles, calls for the three dogs, and sends them inside. Then he turns back to the officer...)

Young Man: Now how can I help you, Mr. Police, sir?

Mr. Dooley: You can start by telling me your name.

Young Man: Now why would I do that? Am I under arrest or something?... You tell me yours first, officer.

Mr. Dooley: Okay, fair enough, *(pulls out his badge and I.D.)* I'm Lieutenant Dooley of the Jackson Police Department... And no, you're not under arrest... yet. Now again, what is your name?

Young Man: Ah-ite, then Lieutenant Dooley, my name is Kenny.

Mr. Dooley: Kenny who? What's your last name, Kenny?

Kenny: Lawson.

Mr. Dooley: Okay Kenny Lawson, would you, by any chance, know someone by the alias name, Squirrel?

Kenny: What you want him for? Did he do anything wrong?

Mr. Dooley: I don't know, Kenny, you tell me. Has Squirrel done anything wrong?

Kenny: Ah-ite, ah-ite, you got me on that one... So what's up? Am I under arrest?

Mr. Dooley: I told you, Kenny, not yet. Again, are you Squirrel?

Kenny: Yeah, man, I'm squirrel. So now what?

Mr. Dooley: Okay, Squirrel, I was told that I could possibly find a juvenile, here at your house.

Kenny: A juvenile? What's that?

Mr. Dooley: That, my friend, is an underage kid hanging out at your house. I'm wondering what you, a grown man, would have in common with a kid.

Kenny: Oh, I see... Would you happen to have a name to go with that juvenile?

Mr. Dooley: Yes, I do... How about Jimmy? Does that ring a bell, Squirrel?

Kenny: As a matter of fact, it does, but he's not here and hasn't been around for a while.

Mr. Dooley: Really? What do you call a while, Squirrel?

Kenny: About a month or so.

Mr. Dooley: Squirrel, I am going to say this and I'm only going to say it once... If I find out that Jimmy is in that house right now, and that you are lying to me, you will be under arrest.

Kenny: For what?

Mr. Dooley: For catering to the delinquency of a minor, for one, and for not having your dogs on a leash, two, and for all this junk in the front yard... Shall I go on?

Kenny: Okay, ok, I get it... Yeah, he's inside.

(Kenny turns and yells for Jimmy to come out. Then the front door opens and out comes Jimmy.)

Mr. Dooley: Hello, son. Are you Jimmy?

Jimmy: Yeah, I'm Jimmy. What do you want with me? I haven't done anything.

Mr. Dooley: Well, let's hope not. How are you doing, Jimmy? Please forgive me for not recognizing you.

Jimmy: What do you mean?

Mr. Dooley: Weren't you just at my house a couple of hours ago, and you mean to tell me that you don't know who I am?

Jimmy: Yeah, I know who you are, you're that... I mean a cop.

(Jimmy is talking this way because he fears Squirrel and wants to confirm his hatred for cops,)

Mr. Dooley: A cop? Is that it, son?... Are you kidding me? You mean to tell me you don't know who I am, only what I am.

Jimmy: Whatta you want me to say, Officer?

Mr. Dooley: *(notices that Jimmy appears to be intimidated by Squirrel.)* Okay, son, it's alright. Are you afraid of this guy, squirrel?.... Is he, by any chance, forcing you to do things that you don't want to?

Kenny: Now wait a minute, what's all this stuff?

Mr. Dooley: Squirrel... Kenny... whatever your name is, I'm going to have to ask you to please keep quiet here. Okay?

Kenny: Ah-ite.

Jimmy: *(stuttering)* N-N-No, I'm not scared of nobody, and I don't do nothing I don't want to do.

Mr. Dooley: Okay, alright, Jimmy. Does your grandma approve of you hanging out with someone twice your age?

Jimmy: My grandma?! How do you know my grandma?! You been talking to her?

Mr. Dooley: Yeah. As a matter of fact, I have been talking to her, Jimmy, and she's very concerned and worried about you, son.

Jimmy: No she isn't, nobody cares about me but Squirrel. (*turns and looks at Squirrel*)

Kenny: (trying to manipulate Mr. Dooley) What's up wit that, Jimmy? Why you dissin' your grandma like that?

(*Kenny is trying to use reverse psychology on Mr. Dooley, in hopes of getting him to believe that he is not leading Jimmy astray, but Mr. Dooley isn't buying into it.*)

Mr. Dooley: Maybe he's dissin' his grandma because, after spending so much of his time with you, Kenny, it appears that, as he put it, don't nobody else care about him.

Kenny: Nuh-uh-uh, Mr. Dooley... You can't blame me for this boy's failures. He was confused when I met him in the street.

Mr. Dooley: Okay. Yeah, you are probably right, Kenny. He probably was confused when you met him, and I guess you were going to make sure that he stayed that way, huh Kenny?

(*After looking on and listening to Kenny and Mr. Dooley fight over his way of life, Jimmy decides to defend himself...*)

Jimmy: (*has tears in his eyes*) Okay, okay already... You all just keep talking about me like I am not here... well, guess what, I am here and I'm leaving now, so you all can finish bickering over me... Seems like all my life, people have been fighting over me.

(Mr. Dooley sees the tears rolling down Jimmy's face and attempts to console him. He walks over to put his arms around him but Jimmy knocks his arm away and yells....)

Jimmy*:* No, don't touch me! You don't know me and you damn sho' don't care about me, Mr. Policeman.

Mr. Dooley: Son, I'm sor... *(Mr. Dooley attempts to apologize but Jimmy turns and runs off)*.

Mr. Dooley: So I guess your rehabilitation tactics were more elevating than everyone else's, huh Squirrel?

Kenny: Well, at least he was not running off like a girl, crying to his mama.

Mr. Dooley: Did you forget? His mama is dead. And who's to say where he's running off to?... We don't know where he might end up.

Kenny: Speak for yourself, I know where Jimmy's going. He's headed straight to Money Mike.

Mr. Dooley: *(perplexed)* Money who?!... Don't tell me there's another twist to all this. I'm beginning to wonder where the climax is here.

Kenny: The what!?

Mr. Dooley: Never mind, son. Just tell me who the heck Money Mike is.

Kenny: You mean to tell me, Mr. Policeman, that you really don't know who Money Mike is?

Mr. Dooley: Why? Am I supposed to?

Kenny: Yeah, I figured every cop in the southeast knew who Money Mike was.

Mr. Dooley: Now why would that be, Kenny?

Kenny: Honestly, Officer Dooley, since and if you really don't know, then I'm not at liberty to say.

(Mr. Dooley is now getting angry and is anxious to catch up to Jimmy, so he has no regard for Kenny's logical reasoning for protecting Money Mike's identity.)

Mr. Dooley: Look, Kenny, I am not in the mood for your street loyalty right now. What I'm concerned with is saving a kid from possible, further harm... So if you are really know where Jimmy is going, I want to know where that is, and I want to know right now.

Kenny: Man, you must be crazy... I am not trying to get myself killed.

Mr. Dooley: Killed?! Is it that serious, Kenny? Because if that's what you are telling me, that this person, Money Mike is in the killing business, then the more I need to get to Jimmy, and soon... So at least tell me where I can find Jimmy; I'll worry about who Money Mike is later.

(Kenny pauses, as if he's giving it some serious thought, and then he commences to tell Mr. Dooley where Jimmy could possibly be found...)

Kenny: Okay, Mr. Dooley, here's the deal... I'll tell you where Money Mike's hangout is, but I won't tell you his real name... And don't you tell him how you located him, and please don't tell Jimmy I told you, because he might tell Money Mike. Okay?

Mr. Dooley: Alright, Kenny, I understand. I'm not trying to get anyone in any trouble here. I just want what's best for Jimmy because he's just a kid, and I promised his grandma that I would do what I could to help her get Jimmy on the right path.

Kenny: Yeah, good... But just what is the right path, officer?

Mr. Dooley: We can discuss that issue a little later, Kenny, if that's okay with you. Right now, I have to locate Jimmy before something tragic happens. Okay?

Kenny: Ah-ite, then let's see... Do you know where the old medical mall is?

Mr. Dooley: Yeah, isn't that over on Beaumont Ave?

Kenny: Yeah, that's it... Well, right behind there, on Laurel Lane, there is a place called M&M's Pool Hall... That's where you can find Money Mike and, hopefully, Jimmy.

Mr. Dooley: Okay, got it. Thanks, Kenny, I'm out of here... I'll be in touch. Here's my card. Call me if, for some reason, I don't catch up to Jimmy and he returns here *(handing Kenny his card)*.

Kenny: *(reaching out to take the card)* Okay, see you later and good luck, Officer Dooley.

(Mr. Dooley gets into his squad car and heads over to the pool hall, hoping to find Jimmy there).

(10 minutes later, Mr. Dooley arrives at M&M's Pool Hall, pulls up into the parking lot, and gets out of his vehicle. As he walks up to the entrance of the pool hall, a couple of guys yell, "Poe Poe!... Yo, poe poe!" as to alert everyone inside that the Mr. Dooley is about to come in.)

(Upon entering the pool hall, Mr. Dooley notices several young guys that look to be around Jimmy's age. Everyone pauses and looks at Mr. Dooley as he steps inside. There is a sense of panic and some people are yearning to get out of the pool hall because they possess narcotics and are afraid of being

busted. So several of the guys immediately exit the building as Mr. Dooley walks over to the counter to inquire of Jimmy's whereabout...)

Mr. Dooley: (talking to guy at counter) Hey, guy, how are you doing? I'm Lieutenant Dooley of the Jackson Police Department, and I'm looking for someone. I was wondering if you could help me out here.

Guy at Counter: Okay, Officer, if I can. Who is it that you're looking for?

Mr. Dooley: Well, it's a little boy... about 5 feet tall, medium build, wears his hair in braids... He's about thirteen years old and his name is Jimmy. I understand that he also goes by the name of June Bug. Do you know him?

Guy at Counter: Yeah, yeah I know June Bug, but I haven't seen him around here today.

Mr. Dooley: Okay. Well, can you tell me the last time you did see him around here?

Guy at Counter: Oh, I believe it was sometime last month... maybe longer, I'm not too sure... but I know its been a minute since Bug came around.

Mr. Dooley: Are you sure about that? June Bug hasn't been here since last month?

Guy at Counter: Yeah, I'm here everyday and I see everybody who comes in here.

Mr. Dooley: Ah-ite, then thanks for your cooperation. Can I ask you one other thing?

Guy at Counter: Yeah, go ahead. What's that?

(Mr. Dooley presumes that the guy is lying to him about the last time he saw Jimmy, but he allows the guy to think that he believes him. He ends that conversation and is now about to throw the guy a curve ball by asking him something that he hopes will scare him into giving up Jimmy.)

Mr. Dooley: Do you know where I can find Money Mike?

(The guy's face contorts with amazement and fear. For he does not know how to answer that, or whether he should respond at all, because no one inside the pool hall recognizes Mr. Dooley...)

Guy at Counter: Did you say Money Mike?

Mr. Dooley: Yeah, that's right, Money Mike... Do you know him?

(The guy *looks over at another guy in the pool hall, as if he needs help answering Mr. Dooley. Then the other guy walks over to Mr. Dooley...)*

Other Guy: Hey Officer, I'm the manager (shakes Mr. Dooley's hand). What's up with these questions? Is anything wrong here? Is this establishment being investigated for wrong doing?

Mr. Dooley: No, nothing's wrong, and the place is not under any investigation. All I want to know is if anybody in here *(looks around the pool hall)* knows June Bug or Money Mike. *(No one responds..)*

Manager: Well Officer, as you can see, nobody in here has any info for you. So if you don't mind, we all would like to get back to business *(implying that Mr. Dooley's company is not welcome).*

Mr. Dooley: Oh, alright, I see... Well, thanks for you all's time. *(reaches over to the guy behind the counter and hands him his business card...)* If you run into June Bug anytime soon, will you ask him to give me a call, please?

Guy at Counter: *(takes the card)* Sure, I'll do that.

(Mr. Dooley walks out of the pool hall and gets into his vehicle. Then another guy from the pool hall comes out and gets into a vehicle as well. Both cars pull off onto the road. As they drive down the street, that same guy pulls up to Mr. Dooley's car and honks the horn to get his attention. Both of them roll down their windows...)

Mr. Dooley: Yeah, what's up?

Guy in vehicle: How you doing, Officer? If you got a minute, I might have some 411 for you.

Mr. Dooley: Okay, pull over into the KFC parking lot straight ahead.

Guy in vehicle: Ah-ite

(The guy and Mr. Dooley both pull into the parking lot, but remain in their vehicles. They pull up beside each other, facing opposite directions, and roll down their windows again. They then begin talking...)

Mr. Dooley: Okay, what's the 411 that you got for me, son?

Guy in vehicle: Well, it's like this... You say that you are looking for your boy, June Bug? I can tell you where to find him, but if I was you, I wouldn't be coming around M&M's asking for Money Mike.

Mr. Dooley: And why is that? Just who in the hell is Money Mike that you feel like I, a cop, shouldn't be inquiring of him?

Guy in vehicle: You mean you don't know?

Mr. Dooley: Know what? That Money Mike is God or something?

Guy in vehicle: Well, almost... They tried to kill him and, three days later, he came back to life.

Mr. Dooley: What in the world are you saying?... Okay, the guy was shot, I presume, and he survived... that happens on occasions.

Guy in vehicle: No, he didn't get shot. He was poisoned, beaten, and left for dead... only he didn't stay dead.

Mr. Dooley: Okay, they pumped his stomach, sewed him up, gave him some medicine, and he recovered... Good medical team work, but no miracle... He's no God, son.

Guy in vehicle: Well, that remains to be seen, 'cause he's untouchable and can't nobody catch him.

Mr. Dooley: Catch him? What? What do you mean they can't catch him?

Guy in vehicle: Just that. He's too fast, too strong, and he always outsmarts everybody. He might be listening to us right now, but I don't care anymore, and I am not afraid of him. I promised my dad, on his death bed, that I would avenge his killer... and I intend to do just that.

Mr. Dooley: Hold on, son, wait a minute now. You are talking about taking the law into your own hands. You can't be telling me this. If, so I would be forced to take you in for conspiracy... so stop talking crazy. Ah-ite?

Guy in vehicle: You do what you have to, officer, but the only way I won't carry out my vow is that I'm dead.

(Mr. Dooley is now more determined than ever to find this mystery man, Money Mike, and is curious as to what relationship he has with Jimmy, if any.)

Mr. Dooley: Okay, young man, enough of that kind of talk... Let me give you my number so we can meet and finish this discussion later. Okay? But for now, can you tell me where I can find June Bug or Jimmy?

Guv in vehicle: That's easy; he's where you just left.

Mr. Dooley: You mean at the pool hall?

Guy in vehicle: Yeah, he was in the back with Money Mike. *(Then, very abruptly, the guy in the vehicle cranks up his car and pulls off...)*

Mr. Dooley: *(yelling) Hey!* Hey, hold on a minute! *(It's too late; the guy has already sped off...)*

(Mr. Dooley looks to his right and spots the manager of the pool hall, across the street, with a camcorder and a zoom in micro-phone dish. After noticing that he has been spotted, the manger puts his camcorder away, walks to his vehicle, gets in and drives off. Mr. Dooley also drives off and heads back to the pool hall to investigate the story of the guy that flagged him down, and to see if Jimmy was really in the back room...]

(10 minutes later, Mr. Dooley arrives back at the pool hall. He gets out of his car and goes inside...)

Guy at Counter: (looks over at Mr. Dooley) I see you're back.

Mr. Dooley: Yeah, and I'm back to get Jimmy... you know... June bug. My understanding is that he is here in the back. If that is the case, then I would advise you to get him out here now, before someone has to go to jail.

Guy at Counter: Now why would you think that June Bug is here, officer, after I....

Mr. Dooley: *(cuts him off)* Yeah, after you lied to me... and you have one minute to come clean, or I'm going to get on my radio and have half the force down here with me going over this place, inside and out. Now even if we don't find Jimmy, we might just find something else that you might not want us to... Do you get my drift?

Guy at Counter: Okay, okay, slow your roll. I'll check again to see if June Bug's around; give me a minute.

Mr. Dooley: Yeah, that's all you have. If you are not back out here in two minutes, I'm making that call, and we will be coming back there.

[The guy walks to the rear of the building and exits through a back door.]

(A minute later, Jimmy and the guy comes out, with a third individual. It is a rather huge guy, who is about 6'8" tall and weighs about 340 pounds. He has a muscular build and is wearing a gold chain, with the pendant of a dollar sign, around his neck. He is very well dressed with black slacks, a black turtle neck sweater, black alligator shoes from Pierre Cardine, and four elegant rings on his fingers. As they all approach, this third person and Mr. Dooley make eye contact, looking directly into each other's eyes, as if to see who will be intimidated by the other. Neither individual gives in. They both hold their own hard looks until...)

Guy at Counter: Okay, I guess I was wrong... 'Looks like June Bug was here afterall. 'Hope you don't lock a brother up for ignorance... Hey, I didn't know.

Mr. Dooley: Well, if you didn't know, you didn't know. *(He focuses on Jimmy)* Hey there, Jimmy... so we meet again. You ran off so fast last time that I did not get to have that talk I promised your grandma I would have with you.
(Jimmy looks over at the strange third guy, as to get his blessings to speak. The guy gives him a nod, as to usher him to go ahead and speak to Mr. Dooley...)

Jimmy: What is it, Officer, that you have to tell me that I don't already know?

Mr. Dooley: Well for one thing, son, you don't know the consequences of your actions as a minor, hanging out here in a place like this. And another thing is that if you should unfortunately, lose your grandma, you will have lost a true best friend, who really cares about you.

Jimmy: No, I don't think so Officer 'cause Money Mike, and the rest of the gang here at the pool hall, shows me much love and friendship *(looks over at Money Mike)*. Aren't I right, Money Mike?

Money Mike: You know what's poppin' here, Little man. When you got Money Mike on your side, you don't have to worry about your back.
(Then he smirks, and Jimmy and everyone else in the pool hall laughs.)

Mr. Dooley: Ah-ite, then Jimmy, 'sounds like you got all you need, and you might feel that you are right. But the fact of the matter is, you're still a minor under the care of Ms. Nuttingham, your grandma. So whether you like it or not, until you're eighteen, son, Money Mike and the rest of the gang will have to take a back seat to your grandma's decision. And right now her decision is for you to come home, refocus your priorities in life by listening to her, and stop hanging out here with these kinds of guys.

Money Mike: Hold up! Hold up! Hold up here, partner! Just what are you trying to say or imply by referring to us as "these kinds of guys"? You don't know me like that to be dissin' me, and you need to check yourself.

Mr. Dooley: Excuse you? I need to what? First off, I am not your partner and you, Mr. Money Mike, don't know me, neither. You the one that need to be doing the checking, because despite your popularity around here, for right now I'm the HNIC... if you know what I mean.

Money Mike: As a matter of fact, Mr. Poe Poe, I do know what that mean, but you are not in charge of jack up in Money Mike's place *(gives Mr. Dooley a straight, stern look in the eye)... So* if you think that you can come up in here and intimidate me with your little tin badge, you better ask somebody... And it don't matter who you ask, because I done put my stamp of approval all over this city... if you know what I mean.

Mr. Dooley: *(while staring back with an even sterner look, walks over and gets in Money Mike's face)* Right now, dog, it's not about this tin badge because I can take it off *(takes off his badge and lays it on the counter).* This is about a vow I made to an old lady, who loves her grandson and wants him home with her for good, and I'm not going to let you... *(turns and points around the whole area of the pool hall)...* and nobody else in here hinder my efforts of putting Jimmy on the right track.

(Jimmy and the others look on in amazement of how Mr. Dooley is standing up to Money Mike.)

Money Mike: *(laughs sarcastically while Mr. Dooley is in his face...)* Nigga, you must be on some good stuff, steppin' up in my face, trying to clown me in front of my boys. What's gonna happen is that, you're gonna find out about the stuff you're putting out... that there will not be enough toilet paper in the whole city to wipe your butt clean of me stompin' it... So if I was you, Mr. Poe Poe, I'd stop selling wolf tickets. You know what they say. Let me see how it goes... Stop giving out checks that you know can't be cashed, or stuff that you don't have enough paper to wipe your butt with. However, if you need to borrow some paper, you can come see me (Money Mike *pulls out a bundle of cash and flashes it in Mr. Dooley's face. Then he and all the others laugh).*

Mr. Dooley: *(reaches out and pushes Money Mike's arm out of his face ...)* If you make another threatening remark to me, Money Mike, by tonight you are going to need to give some of that paper to a bail bondsman, to get you out of jail.

(Everyone quiets down, curious to hear Money Mike's reply...)

Money Mike: Mr. Poe Poe, the day you lock me up is the same day that you'll be signing either yours or somebody close's to you death certificate *(giving Mr. Dooley a serious look).*

(Mr Dooley grabs Money Mike swiftly, turns him around, and puts him in a choke hold...)

Mr. Dooley: That's it; I've had it... You're under arrest.

(Everyone else looks on, wondering if they should assist Money Mike, even asking him what he want them to do...)

Mr. Dooley: I'll tell you all what you better do, and that is step off and mind your business, because if you interfere with my arrest here, I will see to it that whoever steps to me gets the maximum penalty for assaulting a police officer, so if you're that bad... ya'll come on with it.

(Then Money Mike tells his boys to stand down and that he has it under control. He flips Mr. Dooley over his head and onto the floor, while everyone starts to cheer. Then he picks him up over his head and slams him onto a pool table. Mr. Dooley draws his weapon (a 45 magnum) as Money Mike walks toward him, and threatens to blow his brains out if he takes another step. Then there is a big thump and bump at the door... Everyone looks toward the door, including Mr. Dooley. It's Mr. Dooley's back up officers, who have come to assist him. About 10 to 12 officers rush through the door, with their weapons drawn. During this same time, Money Mike decides to make his great escape. Mr. Dooley looks back toward Money Mike and, in a wink of an eye, he dashes out the big picture window, shattering the glass. All the officers fire several rounds of ammunition at the swift moving

target, but to no avail... Not one bullet hit him... and just like that, Money Mike vanishes, as if he is a ghost or magician. Then various individuals in the pool hall begin to talk under their breath... "I told you he was a God... No, a ghost... He's not natural.")

Jimmy:(with a look of glee on his face) I knew it, I knew you all wouldn't be able to take Money Mike in! He's the man!

(Mr. Dooley looks on with total amazement, as does every other officer, except one. That is because the one officer that is not surprised knows about the history behind circumstances surrounding Money Mike's actions... something that all the other officers had just witnessed for the first time. She commences to explain why Money Mike is capable of pulling off such a miraculous stunt...)

Lone Officer: Well, for those of you who don't know the guy that just escaped, he is the late Alfred Kincade... AKA Money Mike. About a year or so ago, he was poisoned, brutally beaten, and left for dead... Actually, according to medical science, he was declared legally dead. Alfred Kidnade did not have any known relatives here and no one ever came to claim his remains, so after hearing about it on the news, Dr. Elenski, a very renowned bionetric scientist, paid to lay Alfred to rest and allegedly had him cremated because of the poison in his system. But the tale of the story is that he didn't have Alfred's body cremated. The word is that he was actually in the middle of some experimental phenomenon, revitalizing dead tissues of human remains with some sort of Bionetric Genetesis tissues that could make the human body stronger, faster, and more intelligent... somewhat of a supernatural being, also capable of seeing and hearing 150 times better than a normal human being. And that guy once worked as a professor at Jackson State University, heading the science lab, but was suspended from the school indefinitely for attempting to get live, able bodies to volunteer for his unrealistic, inhumane idea. After being suspended by the college board's president, Dr. Satcher, he vowed that he would prove everybody wrong and would, one day, avenge his rivals... Some folks even believe that he had something to do with Dr. Satcher's untimely death, but no one was ever able to prove any of that.

Mr. Dooley: Who is Dr. Satcher?

Lone Officer: He was the president of the college board who suspended Dr. Elenski for his inappropriate actions.

Mr. Dooley: Something sounds *very* fishy, cynical and even demonic here to me., but right now I'm exhausted with all that has gone on today and I need some rest....so I am going to head home to get some, but I will get back with you on this Officer Willansby first thing Monday morning, maybe you and I can put our wits together and come up with some answers to all this hoopla... Okay?

Lone Officer: *(Her name being Officer Willansby)* Okay Lieutenant Dooley, sir....I'll see you then, but I am very curious to see how we are going to handle this, considering the enormity of the task ahead.

(Then all the other officers get in their patrol cars and leave... The continued conclusion up next)

**The last time we exited the story, Sergeant Willansby (a fellow officer of Mr. Dooley) had just explained that Money Mike is above average. Dr. Elenski, who is a renowned scientist, had given Money Mike extraordinary upgrades in hearing, sight and, most off all, physical abilities.

Dr. Elenski is also a suspect in the untimely death of Mississippi's former college board president, Dr. Satcher, who passed away shortly after dismissing Dr. Elenski from his position at Jackson State University. Dr. Satcher allegedly died of a heart related complication. However, this story doesn't add up because he had never had any heart problems, prior to his death. As told by a neighbor, a man fitting Money Mike's description was seen leaving Dr. Satcher's residence on the eve of his death. The neighbor claimed that she saw a man run like a bat out of hell, or like a greyhound chasing a rabbit on a race-track. In other words, whoever or whatever it was, had a great running and jumping ability, because the neighbor also said she saw him jump over a fence without even touching it...

(Now it is Monday morning, and Mr. Dooley is in his office at the Jackson Police Department, along with Sergeant Willansby. They are discussing the recent events involving Money Mike...)

Serg. Willansby: As I was saying, sir, one of Dr. Satcher's neighbors, a Ms. Loraine, said she saw Money Mike hop over the fence like a jack rabbit, and that he ran like a bat out of hell.

Mr. Dooley: Well, Sergeant Willansby, if what the neighbor said is true, then perhaps the guy has acrobatic skills. He may have even been a track star, but that's all. Combine all that with a daily scheduled work out habit of weight lifting, and you have your supernatural human being, Sergeant Willansby. I'm sorry... I don't believe in all that stuff you were telling me and the other officers.

Serg. Willansby: Sir, I didn't want to believe it either, and I also tried to theorize all of the possibilities of how that guy was able to do the things I've heard about from different individuals... but all I can come up with is that it's super natural. Anyhow, we've been trying to apprehend Money Mike for six months now, sir..

Mr. Dooley: (with a look of surprise) What?! Six months?! You mean to tell me this guy is a wanted fugitive, and nobody's been able to bring him in?

Serg. Willansby: That's right... not even the U.S. Marshals. I've heard that he has even made the FBI's most wanted list.

Mr. Dooley: What they want him for?

Serg. Willansby: Well, my understanding of the matter is that, about a month ago, Money Mike was at a bar on the north side of town, and a couple of the marshalls caught up with him and tried to apprehend him.

Mr. Dooley: You mean to tell me that two experienced bounty hunters couldn't bring this dude in?

Serg. Willansby: Two?! Did you forget already, sir? Just a couple of days ago, there were a hundred of us at the pool hall... and we still didn't apprehend him. So how on earth were two individuals to accomplish a task that even we couldn't do?

Mr. Dooley: Alright, alright Sergeant Willansby, I get the picture... But it wasn't a hundred of us, it was only thirteen, so we were eighty seven officers short (They both laugh).

(Then Mr. Dooley pulls out the file containing the information on Dr. Satcher's case.)

(After studying the file, Mr. Dooley commences to question Serg. Willansby...)

Mr. Dooley: Sergeant, now about Dr. Satcher's mysterious death... Don't you find it a bit coincidental that he allegedly had a heart attack just one week after Dr. Elenski was suspended from school?... Did they perform an autopsy?

Serg. Willansby: Well, actually, we brought Dr. Elenski in for questioning. He had a solid alibi for his whereabouts the night of Dr. Satcher's death... And yes, an autopsy was performed.

Mr. Dooley: It was?! Then why isn't it here in this file?

Serg. Willansby: That's what I was about to address, sir. The last I knew of it, the findings from the autopsy were still in the files... Why it's not in there now is beyond me.

Mr. Dooley: Okay, then that's where we will start our investigation... I want you to get to the bottom of this ASAP, and I want an answer by the end of the day.

Serg. Willansby: Yes sir, I'm on it right now.

(Serg. Willansby turns and walks out of the office).

*[Then, hoping to get some answers to Dr. Satcher's untimely death, Mr. Dooley picks up the phone, calls over to the university, and asks to be put in contact with whomever is over the science lab. He's now connected to the lab...)

Mr. Dooley: Hello, who am I speaking with?

Lab Person: This is Dr. Olgaston, director of the personnel, science, and laboratory department. How can I help you, sir?

Mr. Dooley: Yes, I am Lieutenant Dooley of the Jackson Police Department, homicide division, and I'm calling you in regards to a case we're investigating on a Dr. David Satcher. I was wondering if you could possibly direct me to someone who might be able to answer a few questions about the incident.

Dr. Olgaston: Well, I'm not sure. Though I am somewhat familiar with what you are asking about, I believe the only one that could assist you would be Professor Jocelyn Greer, who has been overseeing the lab since Dr. Elenski's removal.

Mr. Dooley: Okay, good. How can I get in touch with Professor Greer, ma'am?

Dr. Olgaston: If you would, hold the line please, and I will transfer you to her office now.

Mr. Dooley: Alright, I'll hold. Thanks for your cooperation in this matter.

Mr. Dooley is now being connected to Professor Greer's line...
[Professor Greer was Dr. Elenski's assistant and worked with him in the
lab, but she was unaware of some of the tasks that he undertook, including
that of the Bionetric Genetesis studies. Due to Dr. Elenski's suspension, she
is now director of the Lab Department.]

Mr. Dooley and Professor Greer are now connected on the line together...

Prof. Greer: Hello... Lab Department... Professor Greer speaking.
How can I be of assistance?

Mr. Dooley: Well, ma'am, first I'd like to introduce myself to you. I
am Lieutenant Dooley of the Jackson Police Department, and
I was wondering if I could possibly set up a meeting with you
to discuss some things concerning Dr. Satcher's death and your
former co-worker, Dr. Elenski.

Prof. Greer: Dr. Satcher?! Dr. Elenski?! I'm not sure what you are
asking of me, or even why. Just what... Officer Dooley, is it?

Mr. Dooley: Yes, that's correct, it is Dooley ma'am.

Prof. Greer: Yeah. Just what would I have to discuss with you about
Dr. Satcher and Dr. Elenski?

Mr. Dooley: Well, hopefully, you can shed some light about the
person in question here for me... perhaps something about his
character. After
Dr. Elenski's suspension from the university, was there possibly any
feuding going on between him and Dr. Satcher?

Prof. Greer: Officer Dooley, I don't know what you are looking for,
but I'll be glad to meet with you and discuss whatever it is,
although I don't think I'll be much help, sir.

Mr. Dooley: That's okay; it's just that our investigation was never
completed and we're trying to conclude the case. You see, I

know you might not think you have any thing to help us with, but sometimes what doesn't seem to be much to one person turns out to mean a lot to another. In other words, one man's garbage is another man's treasure, so I'm hoping for the best. Is it possible for us to get together this evening, Professor Greer?

Prof. Greer: Well, actually, I do have a class this evening, but I'm available to meet with you tomorrow morning, if that will work for you.

Mr. Dooley: You know what they say, "Beggers can't be choosers." I'll take it. What time should I be there?

Prof. Greer: Let's say nine-ish, if that's okay with you.

Mr. Dooley: That will be fine, I'll see you then. Thanks for your time.
(They both hang up.)

**It's now Tuesday morning, about 9 A.M. Mr. Dooley arrives at the campus of Jackson State University. After entering the campus, he walks up to the receptionist and introduces himself. He is sent to Professor Greer's office, and is now entering...)*

Prof. Greer: (waiting to greet Mr. Dooley, while standing, with her hand extended) Hello. Good morning... Lieutenant Dooley, I presume?

Mr. Dooley: (shakes Prof. Greer's hand) Yes, and good morning to you, Professor. Thanks for seeing me today.

Prof. Greer: Oh sure, I am glad to be of assistance. Please have a seat.

Mr. Dooley: Thank you (sits down).

Prof. Greer: Now Officer Dooley, as I said over the phone, I'm not sure I can be of much help, but I'll do my best to help you with your investigation. So where do we start?

Mr. Dooley: Let's start with your relationship, or acquaintance, with Dr. Elenski, if that's okay. I'd like to know how long you have known him, and I would like to know as much about his character as possible.

Prof. Greer: Oh, whe... where do I start? You see, Officer Dooley, Dr. Elenski is a brilliant individual. I don't know how much you already know about him, but Dr. Elenski has three doctorate degrees: one in Physics, one in Scientology, and one in Bionetric Genetesis, and he's only fifty years old; that means he has spent over half his life in the classroom, or, library, studying... And he never stops, he's always trying to excel in whatever he does. Be it in the classroom or outside of it, nobody outwits Dr. Elenski.

Mr. Dooley: How so? What do you mean when you say he's always trying to excel? You just said he had three doctorate degrees... What more could he want?

Prof. Greer: Oh, you'd be amazed, Officer Dooley. To Dr. Elenski, the sky is the limit, on to infinity and beyond... and that's putting it mildly, sir.

Mr. Dooley: Yes, I see how much emphasis you put on his hunger for learning and his desire to be at the pinnacle of everything he does.

Prof. Greer: No, Officer Dooley, he doesn't just want to be at the top; he wants to be the one who is totally in charge at the top.., God even.

Mr. Dooley: You don't say!

Prof. Greer: Yes, I did say, and for obvious reasons.

Mr. Dooley: Reasons such as?

Prof. Greer: So I see that you really aren't familiar with Dr. Elenski's passion to procreate a new and diverse human body.

Mr. Dooley: A new and diverse what?!

Prof. Greer: Yeah, you heard right, Lieutenant. Dr. Elenski is very interested in creating a new kind of human being.

Mr. Dooley: Now I've heard it all. You people of the science world are losing it, aren't you? What on earth is he thinking?

Prof. Greer: As a matter of fact, Officer Dooley, you haven't heard it all. And it's not what we people in the science world are thinking here on earth, it's what Dr. Elenski is thinking all by himself... some where out in space. He's trying to conjure up some sort of supernatural human being, but as crazy as it may sound to most of us... believe it or not, Officer Dooley... Dr. Elenski actually has an audience of believers.

Mr. Dooley: Are you kidding me?! You mean to tell me that this nut actually has folks believing his hopeless theories?

Prof. Greer: Now that's where you are wrong, Officer Dooley, I kid you not. His theory doesn't seem to be hopeless. Not only does he have believers, he has actual participants in his experiment.

Mr. Dooley: How could this school, which is supported with our tax paying dollars, allow such an idiotic conjecture to exist, and not do anything about it?

Prof. Greer: That's just it, Officer Dooley, they did do something about it. That's why Dr. Elenski isn't heading the science laboratory anymore, and I was put in charge in his stead.

Mr. Dooley: Okay, then he was fired. His crazy ideas are exposed, and all of this lunacy about him creating a new human is over, right?

Prof. Greer: Wrong... When I said Dr. Elenski was determined to excel, I wasn't joking.

Mr. Dooley: Then Professor, are you saying that, even though this guy has been put out of a job and his work place, this fallacy of his goes on?

Prof. Greer: Exactly... Not only is it still going on, I believe the reason you're here in my office today, discussing this with me, is directly related to Dr. Elenski's endeavors.

Mr. Dooley: How so, Professor? Enlighten me.

Prof. Greer: Think about it, Officer Dooley. Why are you... not a sergeant, but a homicide investigative lieutenant himself... here in my office, at the very university in which Dr. Elenski was fired after Dr. Satcher put his stamp of approval on releasing him which, ironically, may well have cost him his life?

Mr. Dooley: I know that I'm not hearing what I think I'm hearing, Professor. Are you telling me that Dr. Elenski's dismissal from this university and Dr. Satcher's death are both directly related? I hope not, because if so, then it would seem to me that someone has been holding back some serious, incriminating evidence, and if that's the case, someone is in serious trouble.

Prof. Greet: Officer Dooley, I am in no more trouble with your police department than I am with taking over this science lab and not joining Dr. Elenski in his departure... And to be honest, the way things are looking with Dr. Elenski and his endeavors, it seem like I should be more worried about him than your police department.

Mr. Dooley: Really?! So you are telling me that you would rather be incarcerated than to deal with Dr. Elenski's tactics?

Prof. Greet: That's exactly what I am saying, Officer Dooley... Dr. Elenski seems to have a way of making you wish you would have listened to him.

Mr. Dooley: So I guess I am in trouble then, because if Money Mike and Dr. Elenski are in any way connected, then surely by now, I have pissed him off too, by trying to arrest Money Mike.

Prof. Greer: You did wha?!... Arrest Money Mike?!

Mr. Dooley: No, I said I tried to arrest him, and we were unsuccessful for now, but we will get him.

Prof. Greer: If I were you, Officer Dooley, I'd think that over; the idea of apprehending Money Mike.

Mr. Dooley: Now why would I do that, Professor?

Prof. Greer: Because you would be saving countless lives and major embarrassment to your department, as well as rescuing your family from possible endangerment.

Mr. Dooley: Okay, okay, hold on here, Professor... Now you're threading on very thin ice. No one, I mean no one, touches my family... not even
Dr. Elenski, if I have anything to say about it.

Prof. Greer: That's just it... You might have a lot to say about it, but not much you can do to stop it, Officer Dooley. You see, that's how Dr. Satcher got himself killed. You don't want to get on Dr. Elenski's bad side.

Mr. Dooley: Well, you know what, Professor? I just happen to have one of those, too and Dr. Elenski, Money Mike, and everyone else who thinks they can touch my family and get away with it better wake up and apologize before I get angry, because they have not seen anger until one of them touches my family, sweetheart.

Prof. Greer: No, Officer Dooley, it's just the opposite. You have not seen anger until Dr. Elenski has imposed it on you. He has a rather unorthodox way of retaliating.

Mr. Dooley: You know, Professor Greer, I am getting fed up with all this chatter about Dr. Elenski and Money Mike being the big bad wolves of this city. I'm heading back to the precinct to speak with my chief on this matter.

Prof. Greer: Good, I think that would be a wise effort on your part, Lieutenant. However, it will probably prove to be futile for various reasons.

Mr. Dooley: Reasons such as?

Prof. Greer: I'm sorry, lieutenant, I don't care to get into anymore quote "incriminating discussions" unquote.

Mr. Dooley: Professor, why would you use the term incriminating in regards to me discussing this issue with the chief of police?

(Professor Greer gives Mr. Dooley a bright-eyed stare, as to imply, "Read my expression: your chief has his hands in some dirty water".)

Mr. Dooley: Ok, Professor, I'm done here... for now. I will be in touch.

(Mr. Dooley says his good bye and walks off. Fifteen minutes later, he arrives back at the police station. He gets out of his car and goes directly inside to speak with his chief. Mr. Dooley is now entering the building and coming upon the threshold of Chief McClemens' office. Mr. Dooley knocks,

and a voice responds from beyond the clear-view door, "Enter at your own risk." Mr. Dooley opens the door and walks into the office...)*

Chief McClem: Well hello there, Lieutenant Dooley, what can I do for my newest lieutenant?

Mr. Dooley: (smiling) Hello to you, sir... Enter at my own risk, huh? Now what's that all about; we got jokes now? I wouldn't be putting in a resignation from my day job just yet if I were you, sir.

Chief McClem: Oh really? Just what makes you think that I wouldn't make it in stand up comedy?

Mr. Dooley: No disrespect sir, but for one thing, you ain't even good sitting down, so standing up would be a recipe for catastrophe.

Chief McClem: Ok, Lieutenant, let's not get carried away here. Just because you're chief investigator of homicide now, that does not make you a professional comedy scout.

Mr. Dooley: No it doesn't sir, but being a murder investigator, it would be wise of me to stop a crime before it is committed. So I'm sorry... I can't let you go up on the stage,sir... it would be suicide. (They both start laughing).

(Chief McClemens stands up and shakes Mr. Dooley's hand, while they're still laughing. Then the chief motions Mr. Dooley to have a seat, and begins to talk...)

Chief McClem: Ok, Mr. Smart Aleck, state your business before I throw your behind out of my office.

Mr. Dooley: (still laughing) Ah-ite sir, I've told you a thousand times, don't step to me expecting to win unless you're steppin' in front of my coffin, because while there's breath in this body, you don't stand a chance... definitely not sitting down.

Chief McClem: I hear you, Lieutenant... you da man.

Lieut. Dooley: Yeah, that's right, and don't you forget it.

Chief McClem: And don't you forget that I made you the man, so who does that make me?

Mr. Dooley: Let me see, uh... God?

Chief McClem: Now you're talking... and don't you forget it.

(Then the chief and Mr. Dooley puts all jokes aside, and gets down to business...)

Mt. Dooley: Never, sir, would I even consider such a fate. And now that we got all that off our chests, if you would, please allow me to share a rather pressing issue with you.

Chief McClem: And what might that be, Lieutenant?

Mr. Dooley: Well, sir, I don't exactly know where to begin, or whether I should begin it at all.

Chief McClem: Oh, how soon do we forget! Remember, Lieutenant, I'm God so whatever this pressing issue is, give it to me and watch me relieve your pressure.

Mr. Dooley: Ok then, sir, since you put it that way, here it goes... I'm working on a particular case that's rather puzzling, and I don't know if you are familiar with the events surrounding the matter or not, but if you are, perhaps you can shed a little light on it for me.

Chief McClem: Alright, then I'll be happy to, Lieutenant, if I can; but first you gotta tell me what this is all about.

Mr. Dooley: (without hesitation) Sir, it's about the Satcher case over at the campus of JSU, and about a possible suspect in this case, by the name of Dr. Elenski.

(The mere mention of Dr. Elenski gives the chief a look of gloom, as the entire room becomes quiet and cold. Wondering why the chief has such a dull look on his face, Mr. Dooley inquires...)

Mr. Dooley: Sir? Sir, are you okay? Is everything alright?

Chief McClem: Uh... yeah... I'm okay. I just got caught up in a deep thought when you mentioned the Satcher case. You see, that was a rather touching and personal matter to me, Lieutenant.

Mr. Dooley: Really, sir? Personal? And how is that, may I ask?

Chief McClem: Oh, you mean you don't know, Lieutenant?

Mr. Dooley: Know what, sir?

Chief McClem: Dr. Satcher was a half brother of mine.

Mr. Dooley: What?! Your brother?!

Chief McClem: No, Lieutenant, not brother... half brother. He and I had the same dad and different moms, but our dad passed away when we were both just kids.

(Now this has really put a twist on things, because Dr. Satcher was black, but did appear to be of a mixed racial decent. His mom was a black woman; therefore, his dad would have had to been caucasion, but his dad and Chief McClemens' dad, who we have just found out to be one in the same, had passed away some thirty years ago... So the plot thickens here. The lieutenant is now about to respond to the knowledge that

Chief McClemens and Dr. Satcher were brothers.) *

Mr. Dooley: So how long have you known that you and he were brothers, sir?

Chief McClem: Just recently, after Dr. Satcher's funeral. One of my officers, who attended the funeral, knew him and she brought back an obituary. *(The chief pauses...)* *

Mr. Dooley: Aren't you going to finish your explanation, sir?

Chief McClem: Yeah, I'm sorry. This isn't easy, as you may have noticed by now. Anyhow, inscribed within the obituary were references to
Dr. Satcher's parents. *(Chief McClemens pauses again.)* *

Mr. Dooley: And who were named as his birth parents, sir?

Chief McClem: *(yelling in a loud, angry tone)* My dad! My dad! Damn it, Lieutenant! They had my dad's name inside Dr. Satcher's obituary, calling him the son of the late Joseph McClemens and Sarah Belford. Can you believe that? Those sons of bitches had the nerve to disrespect me and my mom and tell the entire city that Dr. Satcher was a bastard kid, and that he was my dad's bastard kid. Do you know how much that hurt my mom and my stepfather, Lieutenant?

Mr. Dooley: No, but I'm sure it was an excruciating pain, sir. No disrespect to your dad, but don't you think he deserves some of the blame here?

Chief McClem: You're God damn right he does! And that's why he's dead... no good son of a bitch.

Mr. Dooley: Whoa, hold on, sir!... Just calm down and lower your voice, please. We wouldn't want the department hearing all this.

Chief McClem: Hell, they already know, Lieutenant. You are the only one that's in the dark here.

Mr. Dooley: Okay, okay fine, sir, but let's not stir things up here. Let's just try and see if we can get to the bottom of all this.

Chief McClem: What are you talking about, Lieutenant? This thing was over until you came along and stirred it up again.

Mr. Dooley: Me, sir? Just how on earth is doing my job characterized as stirring things up?

Chief McClem: Because you've opened up an old, spoiled can of worms, so before the stink comes out, we need to put a lid on it now, Lieutenant... and that's an order.

Mr. Dooley: Sir, you're trying to order me to put a lid on an ongoing investigation?

Chief McClem: That's exactly what I am doing.

Mr. Dooley: I'm sorry, sir, but I can't do that. This is my case. We have a pretty big headway and, besides, it would be unethical and a disservice to Dr. Satcher and his family.

Chief McClem: There's nothing unethical about following orders, Lieutenant, and the only disservice you'd be doing would be to your own family... And we wouldn't want to do that, now would we, Lieutenant?

Mr. Dooley: Excuse me, sir, but am I hearing you right? Are you, indirectly, tryng to threaten me and my family?

Chief McClem: No. Now why on earth would I be foolish enough to threaten you or your family, Lieutenant?

Mr. Dooley: Good, I'd hope not sir, because as you said, it would be foolish... and a big mistake. You see, when it comes to my family,
Chief McClemens, it ain't nothing I wouldn't do to protect them... I mean nothing! *(Mr. Dooley stares the chief in the eye with a look of anger and sincerity.)*

Chief McClem: *(smiling at the Mr. Dooley deviously)* I understand very well, Lieutenant, because I feel the very same way about my mom and her husband... and that's my family. You get my drift? Now this meeting is over, please see your way out of my office *(pointing Mr. Dooley to the door)*.

Mr. Dooley: Okay sir, I'll leave your office, but this meeting is far from over.

Chief McClem: Fine, suit yourself. It's your choice, lieutenant, and if you choose to be a fool, so be it.

(Mr. Dooley does not respond verbally, but he does give the chief an emulative look. Then he exits the chief's office and goes down the hall to his own. He walks in and sits down in his chair, wearing a face of anger and disbelief. And he picks up the phone and dials Sergeant Willansby...)

Serg. Willansby: (answering Mr. Dooley's call) Hello? Sergeant Willansby here.

Mr. Dooley: Yeah, Sergeant Willansby, Lieutenant Dooley here. How are things coming with the investigation of the missing autopsy report?

Serg. Willansby: Well, sir, I was just about to get back to the station and present my findings to you, but since you called, I guess I'll go ahead and tell you over the phone.

Mr. Dooley: No... no Sergeant, don't discuss it over the phone. Where are you right now?

Serg. Willansby: I'm about a couple of blocks away, near the metro-medical mall.

Mr. Dooley: Okay, good. Go there, rather than meeting me here at the precinct, and I'll meet you inside the mall at the Poe Pemp's restaurant.

Serg. Willansby: Alright, sir, so I'll see you shortly.

(Sergeant Willansby and Mr. Dooley both hang up. Then Mr. Dooley heads to the Poe Pemp's restaurant inside the medical mall)

"The Turn of Events Upon The Plot Thickening"
In the story of "Man's Best Friend"
(But The Entire City Loves Him)

Created by
John A. Greer Sr.

Chief McClemens (AKA Joseph McClemens, Jr.) has just told Mr. Dooley that he and the late Dr. Satcher were half brothers. Dr. Satcher was of a mixed racial decent. His mother, who is now deceased, was a young, beautiful, black female named Sarah Belford. For eight years, she had been the live in maid for the late Joseph McClemens, Sr.and his wife (after his death, which was about thirty years ago). Joseph McClemens, Sr. was a white male and was once a big time multimillionaire and commercial real estate developer, who single handedly built a mega empire of commercial real estate and restaurants. This brilliant man first got started by inventing a new shopping cart, which he developed to aid the superstores in moving forward into the new millenium. He called this organization of his, Baskart International Incorporated. Joseph McClemens also started MarVenus, the multi-purpose Mammoth S. A. F. E. Center, and the Poe Pemp's restaurants. His successful building, Allen's International Inventions (A.I.I.), was compiled of many creative minds (ranging from ages eight to eighty) that united to come up with new ventures and ideas that helped move, not only the city but the nation, forward in technological advancement, and is still around today. Joesph McClemens was truly an extraordinary man who relished challenges during his lifetime. Whenever anyone turned him down, although that was rare, it only rallied him to thrust forward faster. He was said to have had a secret, bastard child by his live-in maid, Sarah Belford whose name was David, who would become known as Dr. Satcher. Sarah Belford was pretty smart in her own rights. While studying to become a doctor, she took on her job as a live in maid to help pay her tuition through school. Although she never completed her goal of becoming a doctor, she did make it as far as internship and med-school. Shortly thereafter, she passed away from heart complications. Some people say Joesph McClemens' and her death were related, being that they died only months apart, with him preceding her in death. It was also said that Sarah had more than one child. Some believe that the mysterious child, which was found on her friend's porch three years prior to her death and the bastard child's birth, was Sarah Belford's biological first born, but the true identities of that abandoned baby and its parents were never documented. The talk of the town is that, the abandoned baby was the kid in the news, who was found on the front porch, who grew up, and ran away... never to be found. About twenty-five years later, a mysterious man came into town and landed a job as head of the lab at the local university. Some say that this mysterious man and the mysterious child that ran away thirty years ago are one in the same, and he goes by the name of Dr. Elenski. He has a scar on his left cheek, as did the child, who was very bright and talented. The scar on the left cheek is the reason behind the scepticism surrounding the two individuals.

(Mr. Dooley has just arrived at the medical mall, where Sergeant Willansby is awaiting him inside the Poe Pemp's restaurant. He gets out of his car, walks inside, and is now approaching Sergeant Williansby, who is already seated...)

Mr. Dooley: Hello, Officer Willansby, how are you? 'Hope I haven't kept you waiting long.

Serg. Willansby: Oh, no sir, I haven't been waiting long. Your timing was perfect.

Mr. Dooley: Good, then let's get started right away.

Serg. Willansby: Okay. Can I get you anything, Lieutenant- a burger, coffee, or something?

Mr. Dooley: Thanks Sergeant, I'm not hungry, but I will take a cup of coffee, if you don't mind.

(Sergeant Willansby beckons for the waitress to come over. Then she orders the coffee, and Mr. Dooley begins speaking...)

Mr. Dooley: Okay, then Officer Willansby, what do you have on the case of Dr. Satcher's missing autopsy report?

Serg. Willansby: Yes, of course, sir... What I found is that, the report was taken out of the files, according to Officer Stinson in the records department. He said that Chief McClemens came in about a couple of weeks ago, claiming that he needed to review the files again, but he never returned them to records.

Mr. Dooley: Somehow that doesn't surprise me.

Serg. Willansby: What, sir? The fact that the files haven't been returned?

Mr. Dooley: No, not just that, but the mere fact it was the chief who borrowed the file and did not return it.

Serg. Willansby: What do you mean, Lieutenant?

Mr. Dooley: Well Sergeant, to be honest, something is amiss here, and I'm going to need your fervent effort to help me resolve it. Can I depend on that?

Serg. Willansby: Sir, you know that you can count on me.But whats going on here? Are you telling me that Chief McClemens has something to do with all this?

Mr. Dooley: I'm not certain if he does or not, but having talked to him earlier today has paid its dividends in helping me start on finding out.

Serg. Willansby: I don't know what's going on here sir, and I'm with you all the way, but let's not forget who we are dealing with here... Sometimes Chief McClemens can be down right dirty.

Mr. Dooley: And that's exactly why I'm bringing the Tide concept in on this one, Sergeant.

Serg. Willansby: Tide concept?! What on earth are you talking about, Lieutenant?

Mr. Dooley: Tide, Sergeant, the detergent king... bar none. I intend to clean out all the filth that has corrupted this department and city for years.

Serg. Willansby: Sounds super to me, sir, and I'm down with some good ole fashion cleansing, because with all the corruptions ahead, it's going to take a super heroic effort on our part to battle these evil villains of Jacktown.

Mr. Dooley: Okay, then Robin--- to the bat cave!

(They both laugh at Mr. Dooley's sarcasm. Then Sergeant Williansby replies...)

Serg. Williansby: How come I gotta be Robin? Why couldn't I be Batwoman and you Robin?

Mr. Dooley: Because you use the word holy more than me, Sergeant.

Serg. Willansby: Holy? Just what kind of riddle is that, sir?

Mr. Dooley: It's no riddle, Sergeant, if you think a minute... What were Robin's favorite words?... Holy cow! Holy smoke! And so on.

Serg. Willansby: Oh yeah, sure was!... Now I get it. But what about your character, sir.? Batman, AKA Bruce Wayne, was handsome, rich, and flamboyant.

Mr. Dooley: Oh well... Two out of three ain't bad, wouldn't you say? *(They both laugh and part ways.)*

*(Mr. Dooley gets a call from Mrs. Dooley on his cell phone, informing him that dinner is ready and to not to be late.)**

*(Meanwhile, Serg. Willansby heads back to the precinct, to do some snooping of her own into the Satcher case. This will prove to be a big mistake. For she and Mr. Dooley are being watched and tailed by Chief McClemens' goones.)**

*(Sergeant Willansby has returned to the precinct and is entering her office.)**

(After completing her overtime investigation, Sergeant Willansby turns out the lights in her office and heads out the door. She exits the building and enters the parking garage. Then she unlocks her car's door with a remote and, upon reaching the vehicle, she extends her hand to pull the door open... Suddenly, three masked goons in suits appear, out of nowhere,

with weapons drawn, screaming, "Hold it right there!... Don't move!... You are coming with us, Sergeant Willansby, so just do as you're told and you won't get hurt." Sergeant Willansby immediately surrenders and begins to speak....)*

Serg. Willansby: Okay, Okay, I'll cooperate! Just please don't shoot. What's going on here? What do you want with me?

Head Goon: *(walks up to Serg. Willansby, while unwinding duct tape. Then he uses the tape to seal her mouth and bind her hands, and puts a mask over her head.)*
What we want is for you to keep quiet, and we will ask the questions here.

(About ten minutes later, both vehicles end up at an abandoned warehouse on the south side of town. A huge garage door opens and, as they drive inside, the garage door closes. Everyone exits their vehicles and walks to the rear of Serg. Willansby's car. Then the head goon opens up the trunk, removes Sergeant Willansby, and brings her into the warehouse, where she is greeted by two other individuals. One of them is a female. Sergeant Willansby notices this right away by the sweet smell of perfume and the soft, sensuous voice. Sergeant Willansby is then led to a secluded room inside the warehouse. While following, she wiggles and mumbles, in attempt to speak and find out whats going on...)

Head goon: You might as well keep still since you are already keeping quiet, Sergeant Willansby. *(Everyone else around laughs.)*

(The head goon removes the mask from her head and the duct tape from her mouth. Then he throws her onto the floor of a dark, empty room with no windows...)

Serg. Willansby: Hey!... Hey!... Is this the way your mama taught you to treat a lady?

Head goon: No, but this is how we were taught to teach nosy cops who don't listen when told to. *(slams the door)*

Serg. Willansby: *(banging on the door)* Let me out! Hey, let me out! You can't do this to a policeman!

Head goon: (being sarcastic and chauvinistic) We just did, Mr. Policeman.
(Everyone laughs and returns to their designated duties.)

(Then the head goon walks into an office inside the warehouse. He picks up the telephone and dials a number. The phone rings and a voice from the other end begins to speak...) *
Anonymous voice: Hello... All I want to hear is that you have her.

Head Goon: Yeah, we got her. Did you expect anything different, sir?

Anonymous voice: Don't question me. Just finish your mission and then we will talk. *(The phone clicks--)* *

Head Goon: Can you believe this guy? He hung up on me.

Other Goon: *(in the office with the head goone)* You know, that guy is super strange. That's why I don't want to make him mad, not for a second.

Head Goon: Everybody ain't scared of your Dr. Strange, guy... me, for one, and this other fellow we gotta attend to, Lieutenant Dooley, obviously ain't afraid of him, either. That's why Dr. Strange wants us to rattle his cage, hoping to get him off of his back.

Other Goon: And that's what we are going to do, because I don't want to end up like his brother.

Head Goon: You might be worried about that stuff, partner, but I'm a big boy and I can take care of myself. I'm not doing this because I'm afraid, I'm doing it because I can use the money.

Other Goon: All the money in the world won't do a dead man any good, partner.

(The head goon walks over to the other goon, grabs him by the neck, and picks him up off the floor.)

Head Goon: Repeat that, partner!

Other Goon: *(With a squeaky voice, sounding faint.)* Okay, okay... I'm sorry man, I'm sorry bro....

(The head goon releases his choke hold and pushes the other goon to the floor.)

Head Goon: You are pathetic. You should be scared of Dr. Strange, get out of my office.

(Immediately and frightfully, the other goon gets up and runs out.)

(Meanwhile, back at the Dooleys' residence, Mr. Dooley has just drove up onto his driveway. He gets out of his car, walks up to his front door, opens the door with his key, and walks into his home. Mrs. Dooley greets him at the door, and he begins to speak...)

Mr. Dooley: Hey honey, how are you doing? Sorry I'm late for supper, but you wouldn't believe how unbearable today has been.

Mrs. Dooley: It's okay, sweetie, it's better to be late than not to show up at all. And I'm sorry about your hard day at the office. After dinner, I'll work on making something else hard for you, that I am sure you can put to a better use for the both of us. *(Then she smiles.)*

Mr. Dooley: *(also smiling)* Now that's what I'm talking about, honey. I knew I married the right girl. And it would be alright with me if we skipped the supper and got straight to the dessert.

Mrs. Dooley: *(smiling eagerly in agreement)* You know what? You don't get an argument there because, actually, the dinner is cold. I'm hot, and the kids are away, so this little mouse wants to play.

Mr. Dooley: *(laughing) So you're calling our kids cats, honey?*

Mrs. Dooley: You can call them whatever you want. At this moment, I'm just happy that they are away, 'cause mommy is ready to play.

Mr. Dooley: Well alright, then what are we waiting on?

*(They both walk up to each other and, immediately, the hugging and kissing initiates...)**

*(An hour has passed and the Dooley couple is just about to wrap up their coital affair, when the phone rings. Mr. Dooley reaches out to answer it, and Mrs. Dooley grabs his hand and speaks...)**

Mrs. Dooley: I know you are not going to get that; let it ring, honey.

Mr. Dooley: Honey, as much as I would rather not answer it, I really need to. It's been a very weird day at the office. This might be of importance.

Mrs. Dooley: More important than this? *(removes the cover to expose her alluring body)*

Mr. Dooley: Now that's not fair, honey. That's like comparing apples to oranges... except the phone is the apple right now. And they always tell me that an apple a day keeps the doctor away, and right now I really need to keep a certain doctor away, honey. *(He answers the phone.)*

Mr. Dooley: Hello?... Hello?... Lieutenant Dooley speaking, who's calling?

Voice on other end: Hello Lieutenant, this is Barbara... Barbara Willansby, Sergeant Willansby's daughter.

Mr. Dooley: Oh yeah! Hello, Barbara, how are you?... I'm sorry I didn't recognize your voice. It's been a while since I've spoken with you, but how can I help you?

Barbara: Well sir, I hope I didn't call you at a bad time, but I'm a little worried about my mom.

Mr. Dooley: No, no, it's quite alright, sweetheart. Just what is it about your mom that has gotten you worried?

Barbara: *(starts to cry)* I am sorry for calling you, Lieutenant, and I might be overreacting but... You see, sir, my mom was supposed to meet me at the Poe Pemp's restaurant for dinner about an hour and a half ago, and she never showed up... That's not like her. She has never stood me up, and I am afraid that something has... *(crying while talking)*

Mr. Dooley: Okay, okay, Barbara... Barbara... I'm sure there's an explanation for this, just calm down. We'll get some answers. Where are you now?

Mrs. Dooley: *(is in the background and can hear the hysteria)* Honey, who's that?... Barbara who?... What's going on?

Mr. Dooley: *(shishes Mrs. Dooley and speaks quietly to her)* In a minute, honey.

Barbara: I'm sitting out in the parking lot of the Poe Pemp's restaurant, on my cell.

Mr. Dooley: Alright Barbara, I'll be right there, and we will get this thing sorted out. Okay?

Barbara: Okay, Lieutenant Dooley.

Mr. Dooley: For the record, Barbara, your mom has faced all kinds of adversities in the past and she came through, so whatever this is, I'm certain we all will get through this alright. I'll see you in a few minutes. Just don't leave or talk to anyone else.

Barbara: Okay, but please hurry, I am scared and worried.
(They both hang up.)

Mr. Dooley kisses his wife, tells her that he loves her and that he will explain later, and rushes out the door. Then he gets into his vehicle and drives to the Poe Pemp's restaurant, hurriedly, with the siren on and his lights flashing. *

[Mr. Dooley arrives at the Poe Pemp's restaurant and gets out of his car. He walks over to Sergeant Willansby's 21 year old daughter, Barbara, who is crying hysterically. Then they greet each other with a hug...)

Mr. Dooley: It's okay, Barbara, I'm here now. Settle down, and start from the beginning. Tell me, when was the last time that you spoke to your mom?

Barbara: Let's see... what time is it now? *(Looks at her watch)* I'd say about two hours ago. I was still at work when mom called me and asked if I had any plans for the evening, and I said no. Then she asked me if I would mind meeting her here at Poe Pemp's for dinner. Of course, I said yes, and we both agreed to meet at six o clock, which has been over two hours ago, and I haven't seen or heard from her since, Lieutenant Dooley.
(Barbara is starting to get upset again)

Mr. Dooley: Okay, Barbara, let's not get frantic about this. As I stated over the phone, I'm sure that your mom is okay, and that she has a legitimate explanation for all this. Surely, Sergenant Willansby wouldn't stand you up. Have you tried calling her cell or the office? .

Barbara: Yes, of course, several times... and all I get is her answering service. When was the last time you spoke with my mom, Lieutenant Dooley?

Mr. Dooley: Actually, I believe it was around the same time you did, Barbara. We were both here at Poe Pemp's and she said that she was headed back to the office, to check on a couple of things for a case that we're working.

Barbara: So what do you think, Lieutenant? Would any of that have anything to do with mom not meeting me?

Mr. Dooley: What do you mean?

Barbara: Well, this case that you all are working... you and mom haven't created any enemies, have you?

Mr. Dooley: Barbara honestly, at this point, I don't know but for her sake, I certainly hope not. I'll tell you what, Barbara... Why don't I have a uniform policeman escort you to my house, where you can stay with Mrs. Dooley until I can get some answers?

Barbara: But I...

Mr. Dooley: Please, do it for me and your mom, she would want you to.

Barbara: Alright Lieutenant, I will, but promise me that you will call me as soon as you hear of anything surrounding my mom.

Mr. Dooley: I promise, sweetheart.

(Mr. Dooley radio's the dispatcher and calls for a uniform to meet them there in the parking lot. Shortly thereafter, an officer arrives and Mr. Dooley instructs the officer to escort Barbara to his home, and to remain there until further notice from him.)

Mr. Dooley gets on the phone and calls Chief McClemens to inform him of Sergeant Willansby's strange disappearance.

The phone is ringing and Chief McClemens is answering.

Chief McClemens: Hello? Chief McClemens speaking.

Mr. Dooley: Hello, Chief, it's Lieutenant Dooley here. 'Hope I'm not disturbing you, sir, but I do have a situation here that warrants your immediate attention.

Chief McClem: Okay, Lieutenant. If it's important, let's hear it.

Mr. Dooley: Well, sir, it's about Sergeant Willansby... She's missing.

Chief McClem: What do you mean, the Sergeant is missing, Lieutenant? Missing how?

Mr. Dooley: Just that. She was scheduled to meet with her daughter for dinner over two hours ago, and she never showed up. She's not answering her phone and we haven't been able to get her to answer the radio or locate her anywhere.

Chief McClem: So what are you saying, Lieutenant? Do you suspect foul play here?

Mr. Dooley: It appears that way, sir, and that's why I'm calling you: for permission to pursue this as a missing confidant.

Chief McClem: Okay, Lieutenant, do whatever you deem necessary to get to the bottom of this. Just keep me posted on your progress.

Mr. Dooley: Thanks Chief, I'll get right on it, and I will stress the importance of Sergeant Willansby's safe return to all the other officers. We would want to keep this as low profile as possible and, most certainly, not allow the media to get a glimpse of this.

For it could possibly jeopardise her safety and compromise the advancement of our investigation.

Chief McClem: Right, Lieutenant. I know that I can count on you to proceed with a thorough investigation... and I'll have my secretary to get on this, bright and early, Monday morning.

Mr. Dooley: *(gets offended of the chief's last statement about having his secretary to get on this Monday morning, being that today is Friday)* Yes sir, I will make this top priority.

Chief McClem: Yeah, you do that, Lieutenant, even above that Satcher case, I hope.

{Now Mr. Dooley is really becoming suspicious of the chief's nonchalant attitude toward the Satcher case and Sergeant Willansby's disappearance.}

Mr. Dooley: Sure, sir, Sergeant Willansby is more than just a fellow officer, she has become like family.

Chief McClem: Really, Lieutenant?... That's great. By the way, how *is* your family?

Mr. Dooley: Oh, they're fine, sir, thanks for asking. As a matter of fact, now that you mentioned it, I think I'll give my son and daughter a call
right now; while they are fresh on my mind.

Chief McClem: Yes, you should do that, Lieutenant, because you never know when something could put a halt to that.

Mr. Dooley: What do you mean, sir?

Chief McClem: Oh, nothing in particular, Lieutenant, I'm just speaking generally.
(Now Mr. Dooley is really getting irritated by Chief McClemens' innuendoes.)

Mr. Dooley: Okay, sir, I'll talk to you later, I have to go. I'll be in touch.

(They both say goodbye and hang up.)

{*Mr. Dooley quickly dials Kellie's (his sister-in-law) home, where his son is spending the weekend with his cousin, Mark. The phone rings and Mark answers...}*

Mark: Hello? Hogan's residence, who's calling?

Mr. Dooley: Hello, this is Lieutenant Dooley. Who am I speaking with?

Mark: Oh hey, Uncle Dooley, this is Mark. How is it going?

Mr. Dooley: Well it is going, Mark, but not exactly the way I want it to. Anyhow, I didn't call to bore you with accolades from my job. I would like to speak with Little Jay, please. Is he around right now?

Mark: Yes, sir. As a matter of fact, he is just coming in from outside. Hold on a sec... *(Mark hands Little Jay the phone while telling him it is his dad.}*

Little Jay: Hello? Hey there, dad, how are you doing?

Mr. Dooley: Oh, I am okay, son. What about yourself?

Little Jay: I am fine, dad. How is mom? Is she around?

Mr. Dooley: Your mom is just fine, son, but I am not with her at the moment. Haven't you spoken with her today?

Little Jay: Actually, no... not today, dad, but I was planning to call her in a little bit.

Mr. Dooley: Yeah, you be sure to do that, son.... And next time, do not wait so long to call your mom; that is not a good habit. Always keep us posted. Okay, son?

Little Jay: Okay dad, I am sorry, and I won't wait so long next time.

Mr. Dooley: Good. I was just checking on you all, and I wanted to tell you that I love you, son.

Little Jay: I love you too, dad. Are you alright?...You're acting a little weird.

Mr. Dooley: Yeah, I am alright, son. It's just been a tiresome day; that's all. By the way, when was the last time you spoke to your sister, Diamerald Alexus?

Little Jay: Oh, she and I spoke earlier today, dad... and Diamerald told me that some of her friends saw you on the campus at her school. She hopes that you were not over there to arrest anybody, because she would be embarrassed if you were, so I guess you need to call her and explain why you were there, dad... You know how annoying she can get sometimes.

Mr. Dooley: Yeah, I do. In fact, I was just about to give her a call after speaking with you... but before I go, how is my best friend doing?

Little Jay: I thought you had already spoken with mom.
{Knowing that Mr. Dooley is referring to their dog, Alofus, Little Jay laughs at his own sarcastic remark.}

Mr. Dooley: Okay, you got me, son. Just don't tell your mom that I gave Alofus her identity; she would kill me.

Little Jay: Alright dad, you know I won't, and even though I have Alofus now, you are still my best friend.

Mr. Dooley: Why, thank you, son, that is nice to know... So now tell me, how is our best friend?

Little Jay: He's okay. Mark and I took him to the park to play. He's learned three new tricks, dad... You wanna know what they are?

Mr. Dooley: Sure. What new tricks did Alofus learn today, son?

Little Jay: Alofus can catch a frisbee with his mouth, jump over the bike station's fence depot and... drum roll, please... the third thing Alofus has learned to do is dial 911... Alofus can actually dial 911 on the phone, dad!

Mr. Dooley: Okay, Jay, now what did I tell you about stretching the truth, son?

Little Jay: I know dad, but I'm not stretching the truth. Alofus can do all those things... You can ask Auntie Kellie and Mark; they both witnessed it, too.
(*A bit dubious of what Little Jay claims Alofus can do, Mr. Dooley asks to speak with his sister-in-law, Kellie...*)

Mr. Dooley: Okay son, put your Aunt Kellie on the phone... but hurry, I'm pressed for time.

Little Jay: Alright. Hold on, dad, I will be right back with Auntie Kellie. (*Little Jay calls for his aunt, Kellie, and she comes to the phone to speak with Mr. Dooley, her brother-in-law...*)

Kellie: Hello? Hi there, Jonathan! How have you been doing?... And what is it Little Jay wants me to confirm to you?

Mr. Dooley: Hello to you too, sister-in-law, I'm okay. And how have you been? I'm sorry that I don't get to commune with you all as often as I'd like, but this job and my promotion has kept me super busy.

Kellie: That's okay, Jonathan, I understand. With all the crime going on, I'm glad to hear that someone is hard at work, trying to help keep us safe. Just don't you be discouraged or let anyone curtail your efforts.

Mr. Dooley: Now you don't have to worry yourself about that, sister-in-law. That's one battle I plan to see through, with God's help. However, I don't mean to cut you short, but I'm kind of in a hurry. So can you clarify the validity of Little Jay's Dog, Alofus, being able to dial 911?

Kellie: Isn't that something, Jonathan? A dog being that smart? You know, my sister Lillian and I went to visit Little Jay's dog at the veterinarian hospital when he was just a puppy, and ever since that day, I felt he would grow to be a special animal. I saw it in his eyes when he was lying in that incubator, clinging on to dear life. So I'm not surprised to see him do the things he's doing... even dialing 911. Yes, Jonathan, that dog of Little Jay's is something special.

Mr. Dooley: Alright sister-in-law, thanks, and it was nice talking with you again. I'll tell Lillian I spoke with you. Maybe we can all get together soon to further discuss this miracle dog of Little Jay's. Okay?

Kellie: Okay, Jonathan, you take care and stay prayerful. The devil is busy and he does not care who he hurts.

Mr. Dooley: Alright, I will do that. Now can I speak back to Little Jay, please?
(*Kellie calls for little Jay to come back and get the phone, and he does...*)

Little Jay: Now do you believe me, dad?

Mr. Dooley: Yes, I most certainly do, son... And when you get back home, I am anxious to see those tricks performed first hand. Okay?

Little Jay: Okay, dad... Love you. Goodbye.
(Mr. Dooley tells Little Jay bye and they both hang up. Then Mr. Dooley dials his daughter, Diamerald Alexus, and she answers. He is now speaking to her...)

Mr. Dooley: Hello, Diamerald, how's my baby girl doing?

Diamerald: Hey, daddy. I'm good. How are you?

Mr. Dooley: I'm okay, and I'm glad to hear you say that you are good; let's keep it that way *(being sarcastic)*.

Diamerald: Alright, dad, let's not go there. I am eighteen now, so if I decided to be bad, at least I would not be breaking the law.

Mr. Dooley: Whoa there, Diamerald! That would all depend on what you are doing. If you are smoking a cigarette, you are correct, but if you are drinking alcohol, you would be breaking the law... And if you are engaging in sexual activities, you are definitely breaking the law.

Diamerald: Now dad, I know that it is legal to have sex at my age .

Mr. Dooley: I wasn't talking about the law of the land, I was talking about the law of my hand... because if I found out you were, I would beat your behind the old-fashioned way... by putting you over my lap and spanking you.
(They both laugh [They joke with each other like this because they have an understanding relationship] ...)

Diamerald: Alright dad, you got me on that one, but I will get you back... Anyway, enough nonsense. How is mom?
(She laughs because she knows her dad is about to respond to that statement "enough nonsense".)

Mr. Dooley: Nonsense? What do you mean nonsense? I was playing, but a little serious... I mean real serious, but joking a little. Diamerald, I hope that you are still my little girl... Aren't you?

(Diamerald does not not respond right away. She remains quiet for about 10 seconds, which seem like an eternity to her dad...)

Mr. Dooley: Did you hear me, Diamerald? I said I hope that you are still my little girl.

Diamerald: Yeah, daddy, I am still your little girl... and I always will be, no matter who he is (smirking).

Mr. Dooley: What are you saying? I know you aren't telling me that you're dating when you haven't gotten our approval... Hello?... Hello?... Diamerald, are you there? Answer me.

Diamerald: I am here dad and, no, I am not dating any one. And for the record, I haven't forgotten all the values about life that you and mom instilled in me throughout the last seventeen years. Neither would I do anything to compromise those values, or your trust. I am only focused on getting my degree, not ruining my life. I wouldn't have waited until doors started opening for me, I would have done it when they were shut. In other words, I am thankful to three huge contributors in my life. First of all, I thank God for allowing me to reach eighteen, and helping me to sustain my virginity, rather than ending up cradling a baby out of wedlock or, possibly, contracting some sort of STD, because not only do I love you and mom... and I hope that I am not sounding too conceited... but I also love the beautiful body that God blessed me with, enough not to defile it. I am also grateful to you and mom, dad, for being those doorkeepers those seventeen years. In fact, my earning an academic scholarship was a fruit of you and mom's labor, which allowed the doors to open for me so that I could accomplish my goals... So there dad... now you can focus more on the real crimes that are being commited out there. Okay?

Mr. Dooley: Diamerald, I love you and your brother, and I just don't want you all to have to go down a road of pain and suffering that you should not have to. Just like your heavenly father, I want both of you to cast all your cares upon me. I'd rather carry the heavy burdens so that you and your brother's will be light... For the record, sweetheart, I see all types of things out here in these streets- with adults *and* kids. That is why I pray daily that my kids don't get caught up in it. Do you feel me, baby girl? It's because I love you that I say these things.

Diamerald: I know, dad, and I do understand now that I am older and because I've asked God to help me to understand... not only you and mom... but life itself, and He's doing just that... even as we speak, because to learn of him and his ways are fervent efforts.

Mr. Dooley: Honey, I am so thankful to have a daughter like you, and for the message that you just preached to me. I know now that you will make the right choices... not to say that you won't ever make mistakes, because none of us are perfect... but if and when you mess up, you know who can and will help you right the wrong. I love you, and please keep your family in your daily prayers. I have to go now, darling, but don't forget to call your mom and brother... And we will discuss my visit to your campus later.

Diamerald: Okay, dad, I won't... Love you too. Goodbye.

(Mr. Dooley calls home. The phone rings and Mrs. Dooley answers...) *

Mrs. Dooley: Hello, Dooleys' residence.

Mr. Dooley: Hi, honey, how are you doing? I was calling to check on you and Barbara. How is she doing?

Mrs. Dooley: Okay, I guess, considering the circumstances. What about you? Are you okay? I know all this has got to be taking a toll on you, especially since your hands were already full with that Satcher's case.

Mr. Dooley: Yeah, I know, but it's got to be taken care of. I'll be alright, honey, so don't worry yourself. Okay?.. And tell Barbara that I haven't heard anything yet, but we are working on it diligently.

Mrs. Dooley: Alright, honey, you be careful... and keep me abreast of what's going on.

Mr. Dooley: I will... Just try and keep Barbara as comfortable and as quiet as you can. I'll talk to you later, sweetheart, I'm getting another call here.

(Mr and Mrs. Dooley hangs up- Mr. Dooley clicks over to the other end on his cell phone and answers...)

Mr. Dooley: Hello? Lieutenant Dooley speaking.

(There isn't an immediate response from the other end.)

Mr. Dooley: Hello?... Hello?... Lieutenant Dooley speaking. Can you hear me?... Who's calling?
(Then a deep, faint voice arises on the other end...)

Voice: Never mind who I am, but when I speak, it would be in your best interest to listen, Lieutenant, because warning comes before destruction.

Mr. Dooley: I might not know who you are now, but I will find out after I have this called traced... and whomever you are, you are going to be in a lot of trouble... Now that's a warning before destruction, Mr. Anonymous Caller. Did you forget that you were threatening a cop? In a few minutes, you are going to regret that you dialed my number.

Voice: I don't think so, and if I were you, I wouldn't be making idle threats, especially when you have such a lovely family (starts laughing evilly).

Mr. Dooley: Did I hear you right? Are you threatening my family? Because if you are, I don't take threats lightly.

Voice: Save your measly whining, Lieutenant, you are not dealing with an amateur here. And your best bet would be to just shut up and do as you are told, and then maybe that beautiful family of yours... even that mutt you call a dog... might not get hurt.

Mr. Dooley: If you lay one finger on anyone in my family, I... Hello?... Hello, are you still...

(Then the phone clicks in Mr. Dooley's ear, the anonymous caller has hung up)

(Now Mr. Dooley is very upset and worried about his family, so he calls the officer guarding Mrs. Dooley and Barbara. Immediately after, he calls Mrs. Dooley. The phone rings and Mrs. Dooley answers...)

Mrs. Dooley: Hello, Dooley's residence.

Mr. Dooley: Hello honey, it's me again, I don't have much time so please don't ask a lot of questions right now. I will fill you in on the details later, but I am going to have the officer there to escort you and Barbara to someplace safe.

Mrs. Dooley: But honey... I...

Mr. Dooley: *(yelling)* No! I told you, I haven't got time for questions and answers!... Please, just do as I've asked. Okay? I gotta go now. The officer will handle it, I have already instructed him... I will talk to you soon. Goodbye.

(Mr. Dooley is now calling his daughter, Diamerald, over at the university... The phone rings and Diamerald answers...)

Diamerald: Hello? Hi, dad, what's up?

Mr. Dooley: Hi, baby girl, I am about to give you some instructions, but I don't have a lot of time to discuss this. Okay, sweetheart? So please, just trust me and do what the officers tell you when they arrive.

Diamerald: Officers?!... Arriving here, where I am?!... For what, dad?

Mr. Dooley: As I said, sweetheart, just follow their lead, and I'll explain when I meet up with you, your mom and brother. Okay?

Diamerald: Okay, dad, but now you got me scared and worried. Where's mom and ....

Mr. Dooley: Honey, I don't have time to discuss it. Now please, get your stuff together before the officers arrive... not a lot of things, just your personals.

Diamerald: But what about Hanna?

Mr. Dooley: Who is Hanna, baby girl?

Diamerald: She's my roommate, and I don't want to leave her alone here now... you got me worried. Can I bring her along dad, please?

Mr. Dooley: Okay, bring her along, we will call her parents later... Goodbye, I will see you soon, baby girl.

(Mr. Dooley is now calling his sister-in-law's home, where his son (Little Jay) is spending the weekend. The phone rings and Kellie (the sister-in-law) answers.)

Kellie: Hello? Hogan's residence, where God is good all the time. Who's calling?

Mr. Dooley: Hi Kellie, it's your brother-in-law, Jonathan. How are you doing?

Kellie: Oh honey, I am blessed. Are you calling for Little Jay?

Mr. Dooley: As a matter of fact, I am. Could you please get him for me?

Kellie: Well, Jonathan, Little Jay is not here right now.

Mr. Dooley: *(yelling hysterically)* Not there?! What do you mean he's not there, Kellie?!

Kellie: Wait a minute, Jonathan Dooley. Now I know that Lillian and I look alike, but I'm not her, so you need to tone down that voice of yours and try asking me a little nicer. *(Lillian is the first name of Mr. Dooley's wife. She and Kellie are sisters.)*

Mr. Dooley: Yeah, you're right Kellie, and I am sorry. Please forgive me, but I'm in a hurry and I need to speak to Little Jay right away.

Kellie: It's okay, brother-in-law, I know how the devil can be sometimes, I forgive you. Now about Little Jay, he and Mark left about fifteen minutes ago, to walk that dog of his.

Mr. Dooley: Fifteen minutes, did you say? Do you know which way they were going, by any chance, Kellie?

Kellie: Well, to be honest, I think they were headed back to the park over on Obama Boulevard.

Mr. Dooley: Good, thanks, Kellie. Now could you do me one more favor, love?

Kellie: Well, since you put it that way, Jonathan, I would be glad to, darling. What is it?

Mr. Dooley: Will you please drive down and pick them up for me? It's very important... And when you get back, I am going to have an officer come by to pick you all up and bring you to some place safe. Okay?

Kellie: Jonathan, what's going on?

Mr. Dooley: *(lying because he doesn't want her to panic or alarm the boys)* Everything's okay, Kellie, we're just having an unexpected gathering; that's all.

Kellie: Jonathan, I always hear you and my sister tell your kids not to stretch the truth, and you just stretched the truth so long that it looks like a limo. Now I am willing to help you out here, but you need to be straight with me. Okay?

Mr. Dooley: Okay, okay, Kellie... I'll tell you the whole truth and nothing but the truth, just go pick up the boys and hurry back to your house, please. And I'll talk to you a little later. Alright?

Kellie: You forgot to say, So help me God.

Mr. Dooley: What? What on earth are you talking about, Kellie?

Kellie: When you said that you would tell me the whole truth and nothing but the...

(Mr. Dooley interrupts her...)

Mr. Dooley: Kellie, sweetheart, I know that you are a very religious individual, but right now this is serious business; it could be a matter of life or death. So will you please just do what I asked you, dear?

Kellie: Alright Jonathan, I'm sorry, I didn't know. I am on my way out the door right now.

Mr. Dooley: Good, I'll talk to you soon.

(They both hang up. Then Mr. Dooley orders a couple of squad cars to his sister-in-law's home.)

(Meanwhile, Mr. Dooley awaits a return call from his sister-in-law, Kellie. Instead, he gets another anonymous call, and he answers...)

Mr. Dooley: *(answering with presentiment)* Hello? *(voice is faint so he repeats it)* Hello?... Lieutenant Dooley here.

Voice: Well, well, well- if it isn't Mr. Hardhead himself. How are you and the family doing?

Mr. Dooley: I told you to leave my family out of this. If you got a problem with me, deal with me. I will meet you whenever or wherever you want me to.

Voice: Let's just say that you have been warned one more time, Lieutenant. Remember... next comes the destruction.

Mr. Dooley: What are you talking about? Who am I speaking with? Do you ... *(phone hangs up)* Hello?... Hello?... Do you know anything about Sergeant Willansby?... Hello?...

(Mr. Dooley pauses to catch his breath and is now sitting quietly. The phone rings again and he answers it on the first ring this time...)

Mr. Dooley: Hello?... Hello... Where is Sergeant Willansby?

(Mr. Dooley hears the voice of a child who appears to be crying...)

Child Voice: Daddy, daddy, they took Alofus? They took Alofus, daddy. Why?...

Mr. Dooley: Is that you, Little Jay? What's going on, son?... Settle down, Little Jay. It's okay, son... Settle down and tell dad what's going on so I can help. Alright, Little Jay?

Little Jay: Alright, dad. Mark and I were walking Alofus on our way to the park, over on Obama Boulevard. Then a truck pulled up and all these guys jumped out, yelling and screaming at me and Mark. We didn't know what to do, dad... *(starts to cry again)**

Mr. Dooley: Son, it's okay, now... It's okay... Dad is going to make it alright, and you did the right thing, son. Just settle down and finish telling me what happened.

Little Jay: As I was saying, dad, Mark and I were walking Alofus to the park and these guys pulled up beside us in a truck.

Mr. Dooley: Are you sure it was a truck, son?... Like dad's pick up or was it like the postman's truck?

*(The postman's truck is a van.... Mr. Dooley's truck is a pick-up with a flatbed.)**

Little Jay: It was like the postman's truck, only bigger.

Mr. Dooley: Okay, you're doing good, son. Now can you remember what color the vehicle was, or anything else that would help describe it?

Little Jay: I believe it was blue, and it had some kind of logo and writing on the sides... I'm sorry, dad, that's all I can remember. It happened so fast and I was scared... Mark is right here with me and he wants to talk to you.

Mr. Dooley: Put him on the phone, son.

Mark: Hello, Uncle Dooley.

Mr. Dooley: Hi, son, are you okay?

Mark: Yes sir, I'm alright, I was just scared for Alofus.

Mr. Dooley. What do you mean? Why were you scared for Alofus?

Mark: Well sir, you see, Alofus was really trying to protect me and Little Jay, and for a little while, he was winning. He bit one of the guys in the butt. Then he jumped on another one and was biting at his face, but the guy started choking him. Then Alofus got loose from him and started running toward the other guy he bit in the behind. But before Alofus could get to him, some other guy got out of the truck with a big hook and grabbed him by the head and neck, and threw him up into a cage in the back of the truck. Then all the other guys got in the truck and they drove off.

Mr. Dooley: Thanks, Mark, you've been real helpful, son... One other thing; were you able to see the license plate of the truck?

Mark: No, not really. It all happened so fast, but I do remember the picture and the writing on the side, sir.

Mr. Dooley: You do?! What was it, Mark?

Mark: It was a picture of a man with a hammer and some other sort of tools... and the words on the truck read "We let our work do the talking for us".

Mr. Dooley: Are you sure about that? Is that all you remember, Mark?

Mark: Yes, sir... Oh! One other thing I remember, Uncle Dooley...

Mr. Dooley: Yeah, what's that?

Mark: The guy who got out of the truck was bigger than all the other guys, and one of the guys called his name by accident.

Mr. Dooley: Why would you say that it was an accident, Mark?

Mark: Because after he said his name, the big guy gave him this certain look.

Mr. Dooley: What look, son?

Mark: The same look my dad used to give me when I said something he didn't like in public. It was the look to let me know that I was in trouble when we got back home.

Mr. Dooley: Okay, good. What name did the guy call the bigger guy, Mark?

Mark: He called him Money Mike.

Mr. Dooley: Are you sure, Mark?! This is very good information!

Mark: Yes sir, I remember, because after he called his name, the big guy looked over at me and started walking toward me and Little Jay, but that's when mom pulled up, blowing her horn.

Mr. Dooley: Your mom's there?

Mark: Yeah, that's how we are calling you. Mom let Little Jay use her cell phone to call you.

Mr. Dooley: Put her on the phone.

Mark: Okay.

(Kellie (Mark's mom) is on the phone.)

Kellie: Hello, Jonathan, this is Kellie. Do you have any idea what all this is about?

Mr. Dooley: Hi, Kellie, are you and the boys okay? Are either of them hurt?

Kellie: As far as I can see, they're okay, just a little frightened... But what about my question, Jonathan? Does any of this have anything to do with you wanting me to pick them up?

Mr. Dooley: Not right now, Kellie, please... not in front of the kids. And honestly, I'm not sure yet. However, two of my officers will be arriving there shortly. I want you and the boys to go with them. Okay?

Kellie: Alright, Jonathan. I'm going to trust you on this one, but will we see you and Lillian later?

Mr. Dooley: Yeah, real soon. I have a couple of things to attend to, but I will meet up with you all shortly. Goodbye.

(They both hang up... Mr. Dooley is already en route to the park on Obama Boulevard, where Alofus was abducted. He has called the crime-scene investigative unit to meet him there and see if they can get more evidence, or interview potential witnesses.)

**(A short while later, Mr. Dooley arrives at the park. The crime scene unit and several other squad cars are already on the scene. Mr. Dooley gets out of his vehicle, and is then greeted by one of the sergeants in the crime scene unit, Sergeant Ortega...)*

Serg. Ortega: {is a Hispanic male} Hello, Lieutenant Dooley. How are you, sir? I'm Sergeant Ortega, with the crime scene unit.

Mr. Dooley: Hello, Sergeant Ortega, what do we have here?... Anything?

Serg. Ortega: Well, sir, we've only been here a couple of minutes, but we did notice some skid marks. A couple of the officers are pouring the mix now, in order to get samples of the tire traction, and we also found pieces of garments... 'Don't know if that's anything, though.

Mr. Dooley: Good, keep at it Sergeant, I don't want you all to leave a leaf unturned. Check for shoe tracks, chewing gum, or even spit on the ground. I want all of it analyzed for DNA samples ASAP.

Serg. Ortega: Yes, sir, but really sir- chewing gum, shoe tracks? Don't you know how many people walk this park daily?... Thousands perhaps.

Mr. Dooley: Sergeant, I wouldn't care if it was millions... And about the gum and tracks, I meant it. You are to treat this case as if it was one of our own. Is that understood?

Serg. Ortega: Yes, sir, right away

(Mr. Dooley walks away before Sergeant Ortega responds. He walks upon another officer, a female corporal named Corporal Davenport, who he is now speaking to. Quite a few bystanders have gathered in the park...)

Mr. Dooley: Hi there, Corporal... Lieutenant Dooley, with homicide. I would like for you to keep these people away from the area we've designated to investigate. As a matter of fact, section off this entire block. Then I want you to see if there are any potential witnesses to this matter. Okay?

Corp. Davenport: {is a black female} Okay, Lieutenant, I'll get right on it. By the way, sir, I heard that your son and nephew were the victims. Are they okay?

Mr. Dooley: Yes, Corporal. Fortunately, they are okay, just a little upset and frightened... The perpetrators also took my son's dog.

Corp. Davenport: They did what, sir? Took your dog?! Why would anyone want to kidnap someone's dog?

Mr. Dooley: I don't know, Corporal, but that's why we're here, hoping to find out- so let's get to it.

Corp. Davenport: Yes, sir. (turns and walks toward the crowd...) Alright, move back so we can canduct this investigation... Has anyone here seen any strange events occuring in the park today? If so, please step forward so that I can get your statements.

Meanwhile, Lieutenant Dooley walks off and calls Mrs. Dooley on his cell phone to speak with her... The phone rings and Mrs. Dooley now answers...

Mrs. Dooley: (has already heard about Alofus' abduction) Hello, honey, tell me it ain't true.

Mr. Dooley: I would like to, sweetheart, but unfortunately it is true... But don't you and the kids worry, we will get to the bottom of all this mess, and we will get Alofus back.

Mrs. Dooley: Honey, I hear you and I want to believe you, but honestly, I am beginning to get a little pessimistic about all that has happened... You know, with Sergeant Willansby being missing, our baby being harassed, and now Alofus being kidnapped... What's next, honey? What's really going on here, or do you not have an answer yourself?

Mr. Dooley: Well, I understand your pessimism, sweetie, and I don't blame you for being frightened and worried... And no, I don't have an answer for it yet, though I do have a clue as to who is behind all this, but I'm not saying just yet for fear of jeopardizing the investigation. Okay, love? I gotta go now, but I'll be in touch. Alright?

Mrs. Dooley: Alright sweetheart, you be extra careful, and please don't underestimate whomever this idiot is, because if they are willing to threaten you-a cop- and your child, as well as kidnap Sergeant Willansby and Alofus, then something is very amiss here. So honey, please don't forget that we all love you and we need you to come back home to us. Okay?

Mr. Dooley: Don't you worry, darling, you just take care of the kids and console Barbara. I am going to get to the bottom of this... And by the way, Diamerald, her roommate, your sister Kellie, her son Mark, and Little Jay should be joining you all soon. Make them all comfortable. I'll talk to you a little later, goodbye.

****(*Mrs. Dooley says her goodbye and they both hang up. Mr. Dooley gets an incoming right after his conversation with Mrs. Dooley--*
It's Chief McClemens. Mr. Dooley is now answering the phone.)**

Mr. Dooley: Hello, Lieutenant Dooley here, who's calling?

Chief McClem: Hello there, Lieutenant, what's going on? This is Chief McClemens. What is this about your son and nephew being abducted?

Mr. Dooley: No sir, my son and nephew weren't abducted. However, they were harassed, and my son's dog has been kidnapped.

Chief McClem: What?! Your son's dog has been kidnapped?!... Am I hearing you correctly, Lieutenant?

Mr. Dooley: Yes sir, you are, and we are somewhat baffled on this one ourselves, but I'm on it and I am going to get to the bottom of it.

Chief McClem: I know that you will, Lieutenant, I would never expect anything less. That is why I had you promoted. You are a superb officer. Feel free to call me if you warrant any more of my assistance, Lieutenant. Okay?

Mr. Dooley: Yes sir, I would be sure to do that.

Chief McClem: Is your son and nephew okay, Lieutenant? And do you have any possible leads?

Mr. Dooley: Yes, they are okay, and no, not just yet on any leads, sir, but you can bet your bottom dollar we will get the perpetrator that's responsible for this and Sergeant Willansby's disappearance.

Chief McClem: Sergeant Willansby, Lieutenant?... What, do you believe they are connected?

Mr. Dooley: Yes sir, I do, I believe the culprit of this matter and Sergeant Willansby's abduction are one in the same.

Chief McClem: What, exactly, what would make you think such a thing, Lieutenant?

Mr. Dooley: Well, because of the strange phone calls and threats that I've received, sir... Also, because of the timing involved. I don't believe it's no coincidence that both my dog and Sergeant Willansby would come up missing hours apart.

Chief McClem: Yeah, it seems like you might have something there, Lieutenant. Okay, I am going to let you go now, so that you can get on with this investigation. Again, just keep me posted. Alright?

Mr. Dooley: Alright, sir. *(Mr. Dooley says his good bye and they both hang. Immediately after, a uniform officer named Officer Bradley runs up to Lieutenant Dooley, in a panic...)*

Ofc. Bradley: {is a white male} Lieutenant... Lieutenant... Sir, we... *(The officer is almost out of breath from running over to tell Mr. Dooley the news.)*

Mr. Dooley: Hold on there, fellow, just calm down and tell me what it is.

Ofc. Bradley: *(settles down and catches his breath)* Sir, we think that we have located your missing...

* *(Mr. Dooley gets excited, hoping that the officer is about to tell him that they have located Sergeant Willansby, so he completes the sentence...)*

Mr. Dooley: Sergeant Willansby... you all have found her?

Ofc. Bradley: I am sorry sir, but no, we haven't found Sergeant Willansby. However, we do believe that we have located your missing dog, sir.

Mr. Dooley: Alofus?! Really?! Where?!

Ofc. Bradley: Well sir, Officer Lansing called over the radio and said that he came up on what appeared to be a bundle of clothes, just lying on the side of the road, halfway in the street. So he got out to investigate and found that the object that he thought to be a bundle of clothes was actually a dog that lay wounded... wounded very badly, sir.

**(Mr. Dooley cuts the officer short again...)*

Mr. Dooley: He is okay, isn't he? I mean, he's not dead, is he?... Please don't tell me he's dead.

Ofc. Bradley: Honestly, I don't know sir, that's all I got. I was instructed to get you this information and take you where the dog is.

Mr. Dooley: Where? Where is he, Officer?

Ofc. Bradley: According to Officer Lansing, about a mile east of here, sir... over on Clinton Boulevard, near the old Vicksburg over-pass.

Mr. Dooley: Okay, good, let's go.

**(Mr. Dooley and Officer Bradley get into their vehicles and head to Alofus' alleged location...)*

*(Minutes later, Mr. Dooley and Officer Bradley arrive at the scene, where Alofus was found wounded. They both get out of their vehicles and start walking toward the wounded dog. Mr. Dooley is greeted by Officer Lansing, who was on the scene first, and they begin speaking...)**

Ofc. Lansing: {is a white male} *(extends his hand to shake Mr. Dooley's hand)* Hello... Lieutenant Dooley, I presume?

Mr. Dooley: (shakes Officer Lansing's hand) Yes, and you are?

Ofc. Lansing: I am Officer Lansing, sir. I found the dog here, in the street, in the condition told to you.

Mr. Dooley: Upon locating the dog did you, by any chance, see any one walking or driving off, Officer Lansing?

Ofc. Lansing: No. sir. I did not. As a matter of fact, the entire block here was vacant, as it usually is this time of day.

Mr. Dooley: So I guess whoever dumped the dog here knew this, and that's probably why they chose to drive him here. *(Mr. Dooley and the other officers walk toward Alofus. Mr. Dooley is now kneeling down, to check on the dog's condition. Alofus is barely alive with a faint pulse. He has been beaten severely and has trauma to the head, his hind legs are broken, and one of his eyes have been punctured.*

**(Mr. Dooley has tears in his eyes, as does Officer Bradley.)*

<u>Mr. Dooley</u>: *(rubbing the dog's head)* I'm sorry boy, I'm so sorry, but I promise you we will get whoever did this to you. Just hang in there, boy, we are going to get you some help.

(Mr. Dooley turns to Officer Bradley, and asks him to get on the radio and get a vet down there.)

Ofc. Bradley: Yes, sir. *(Officer Bradley gets on his 2-way and calls for the dispatch to get an ambulatory vet to the scene ASAP.)*

(Meanwhile, Mr. Dooley is still attending to Alofus, while rubbing his head and trying to console him. Alofus miraculously opens his one good eye and tries to hold his head up. Mr. Dooley tries to keep him still, telling him not to move, but Alofus is insistent upon giving him a sign that it isn't over and to not give up on him. Alofus even raises his front leg, as to give Mr. Dooley a paw to hold on to. While all this is going on, a vehicle pulls up with inscriptions on the side that read "Metro Area Veterinarian Ambulatory Service Hospital, a 24 hour facility". A couple of people exit the vehicle and take out a cart with wheels. They rolls the cart over to Mr. Dooley and Alofus. One of the individuals has on a unique type of scrub and badge. He walks up to the Mr. Dooley and kneels down beside him, as to console him. He tells Mr. Dooley to let him handle it from here. The individual is a veterinarian doctor named Dr. Smortzen, who is now speaking...)

Dr. Smortzen: *(with his arm around Mr. Dooley's shoulder))* Hi there, Officer, I am Dr. Smortzen and I'm with M.A.V.A.S.H. Is this your dog, sir?

(Lieutenant Dooley has now gotten up to leave the vet to tend to Alofus, and is now responding to the doctor's question.)

Mr. Dooley: Well, yes and no, Dr. Smortzen. You see, he actually belongs to my son, but I guess that technically makes him mine.

Dr. Smortzen: Yeah, I would say so... Anyhow, what's your name, so I won't have to keep referring to you as Officer?

Mr. Dooley: Okay, good enough... I am Lieutenant Dooley, Dr. Smortzen. So how does it look? Is my dog going to be alright?

Dr. Smortzen: Well, I can't tell just yet, Lieutenant. Give me a minute or two here and I will try and get a prognosis for you... By the way, what is the dog's name?

Mr. Dooley: Alofus, his name is Alofus.

Dr. Smortzen: Did you say Alofus, Lieutenant?

Mr. Dooley: Yes, that is correct, Doc.

Dr. Smortzen: (while still examining the dog) That's a rather unique name, Lieutenant, and I like it. How long have you all had the dog, and how did that name come about?

Mr. Dooley: Why, thank you Dr. Smortzen. I thought the name was unique myself. As a matter of fact, my son came up with it. He said it was given to him in a vision from God.

Dr. Smortzen: *(laughs)* From God, Lieutenant?

Mr. Dooley: Hold on, Doc... Always hear the whole sratement before you make a conclusive judgment. You see, this dog that you are nursing is a very special animal. He was given to my son, Jonathan Jr., for his eleventh birthday, about a year ago... His grandparents gave it to him. They had a dog that gave birth to six puppies, and five of them died. This dog was the lone survivor. He was a fighter. He stayed on life support in an incubator for a month and a half, I believe, but he made it through. The entire city here rallied behind his efforts to live, and...

(Dr. *smortzen interrupts Mr. Dooley...*)

Dr. Smortzen: You mean to tell me this is him?

Mr. Dooley: What are you talking about, Dr. Smortzen?

Dr. Smortzen: I'm asking if this is the puppy that everyone loved and wanted to adopt.

Mr. Dooley: I don't know nothing about anyone wanting to adopt Alofus Doc, but yes, he is the one everyone rallied to help save his life and, ironically, here we are again a year later, trying to save his life again... I guess history really does repeat itself, huh Doc?

(Almost immediately, the look on Dr. Smortzen's face becomes a look of desperation and determination, and the calamity stops. He calls his assistant over for help and tells him that they need to hurry and get the dog to the hospital right away...)

Dr. Smortzen: Excuse me, Lieutenant, but we have a miracle dog here that we gotta save.

(He gets on his cell and calls the hospital to tell them to prep the operating room, because they're on their way. Then he puts an oxygen cup over Alofus' mouth, bandages his head, and splints his hind legs. After doing so, he lifts Alofus onto the cart, and puts him into the van. He tells Mr. Dooley where he's taking Alofus and Mr. Dooley tells him that he will be there after he gets in touch with the rest of the family. So Mr. Dooley calls his wife, Mrs. Dooley... The phone rings and Mrs. Dooley answers...)

Mr. Dooley: Hello, sweetie, its me. I have some good news for you all... and some bad news. The good news is that we found Alofus.

(Mrs. Dooley gets all excited and screams to the others, "He found Alofus! He found Alofus, ya'll!" Then everyone else rejoices, while Mr. Dooley is hearing all this excitement in the background... Finally, after things settle down, Mr. Dooley speaks...)

Mr. Dooley: Honey... Honey, listen to me. As I said, yes we did find Alofus, but there is also some bad news.

Mrs. Dooley: I know honey, I heard you. It's just that we haven't heard any good news for so long that I thought we should relish that moment;
that's all. Now go ahead, tell me the bad news.

Mr. Dooley: Well uh... You see, Alofus uh...

Mrs. Dooley: Honey... Honey, will you please stop it with the *uh* already... Just tell me the bad news. Okay?

Mr. Dooley: Okay, sweetie, okay... Alofus is hurt, and he is hurt very badly.

Mrs. Dooley: How bad?

Mr. Dooley: Bad enough that he has to have surgery, and he might not make it.

** *(Overhearing the conversation, Little Jay, Mark and Diamerald all stand next to Mrs. Dooley, questioning her while she is still on the line with Mr. Dooley, so Mrs. Dooley gets quiet for a moment)*

Mr. Dooley: Hello?... Hello?... Honey, are you still there?... Hello?

Mrs. Dooley: Yes honey, I'm still here, and so are Little Jay and Diamerald; they're waiting to speak to you.

Mr. Dooley: I understand, sweetheart, put them on the phone. *(Mrs. Dooley hands the phone to Little Jay.)*

Little Jay: Hi, dad! Is Alofus alright? I heard mom ask how bad something was. Tell me, dad, is he okay?... And please don't stretch the truth about it, please dad.

Mr. Dooley: Alright, son, you want me to give it to you straight?... Alofus is hurt- he's hurt bad, and he needs surgery right away.

Little Jay: (crying while speaking) Surgery?!... Surgery, dad?! What did they do to Alofus?

Mr. Dooley: Well son, they beat him up pretty bad, and he might have lost one of his eyes, but we don't know just yet. He's headed to the vet right now, and he has a good doctor, Dr. Smortzen... I've talked with him. And we all know that Alofus is a fighter, so all we can do right now is pray for him. Okay? It's going to be alright, just keep the same faith we all had when Alofus was hurt before as a puppy.

Little Jay: *(still weeping)* But dad, why would anybody want to hurt Alofus? Why, dad, why?!

Mr. Dooley: I don't know, son. All I can say is, there's just evil folks in this world and, perhaps, one day God will give all of us an answer. Okay? Now you stop worrying yourself before you get sick and you won't be able to run and play with Alofus when he gets well. Okay, son?

Little Jay: Alright, dad.

Mr. Dooley: I love you Little Jay, and so does Alofus... he told me. When I mentioned your name, he handed me his paw.

Little Jay: He really did that, dad? You promise?... And you are not stretching the truth?

Mr. Dooley: Yes, he did Little Jay, and I am not stretching the truth. Now you take care, and let me speak with your sister now. Okay?

Little Jay: Okay, dad... Love you. *(Then he hands Diamerald the phone.)*

Diamerald: Hi, dad, are you okay?

Mr. Dooley: Yeah, sweetie, dad's okay. How are you holding up, with all that's going on here?

Diamerald. Well, I am sad to hear what has happened to Alofus, and to see how hard Little Jay is taking it, dad, but I am trying to stay strong for mom and Little Jay. I remember you telling me to stay strong for them after NaNa and Paw Paw died, so I feel that I have to do it again.

Mr. Dooley: Honey, you are one in a million and I am so thankful to have a daughter like you, but it's okay for you to cry... I even cried today when I saw Alofus in that condition.

Diamerald: Really dad? You cried?

Mr. Dooley: Yeah sweetheart, daddy is human too, even though you all think that I'm a robot at times.

Diamerald: A robot can have feelings, dad.

Mr. Dooley: What?... A robot can have feelings? Diamerald, what science fiction novel have you been reading, sweetheart?

Diamerald: No dad, it's true, and it's not science fiction any longer. This is part of my studies over at the university... We are studying Bionics in its infant stage.

Mr. Dooley: Honey, I am glad to hear that our money is not being wasted, and to see that you are actually learning something worthwhile, but we will have to finish this conversation at a later date. Okay?

Diamerald: Okay dad, I love you, and you be careful... Here's mom. Goodbye. *(Mrs. Dooley takes the phone again and begins to speak.)*

Mrs. Dooley: Hi honey, I don't know what you said to Little Jay- but whatever it was, I'm glad because he seems to be at ease for the moment... And what were you and Diamerald talking about? I overheard her mention something about science fiction and Bionics... What's with that conversation?

Mr. Dooley: Just something about her studies at the school, honey. Anyhow, I told her that we would finish that conversation at a later date, so enough of all that. I'm going to instruct the officers there to bring you all to the M.A.V.A.S.H; I'll meet you there.

Mrs. Dooley: M.A.V.A.S.H?... What's that, honey?

Mr. Dooley: Oh I'm sorry, that's an abbreviation for the Metro Area Veterinarian Ambulatory Service Hospital. It's for animals, and Alofus is there. I want you all there while he undergoes his surgery. Okay?

Mrs. Dooley: Okay, sweetheart, we'll meet you there shortly. Goodbye.

(They both hang up and everyone heads to the M.A.V.A.S.H.)

**(Mr. Dooley arrives at the M.A.V.A.S.H. first. He gets out of his car and walks inside. After entering the facility, he walks over to the receptionist to inquire of Alofus' whereabouts. He also asks to speak with Dr. Smortzen. The receptionist is now responding to Mr. Dooley's questions...)*

Recept: Yes, officer, we do have your dog, Alofus. They just took him down the hallway to prep him for surgery... you know, cleaning him up, giving him anesthesia... and if you will just have a seat over there in the waiting room, I will page Dr. Smortzen to see if he can come out and speak with you. Okay?

Mr. Dooley: Okay, ma'am, thank you and I appreciate your immediate assistance.

Recept: Oh, you're welcome Officer uh... uh... could I get your name
again? I seemed to have forgotten it.
(Gives him a pen and a pad) Here, if you will, just write down some
brief info on this pad for me so when Dr. Smortzen calls me back, I'll
know what to tell him.

*(Mr. Dooley writes down his name, Alofus' name, and his reason for being
there. He then gives the notepad to the receptionist. She thanks him and he
walks into the waiting room. About fifteen minutes later, Mr. Dooley gets
a call on his cell phone, and he answers it...)*

Mr. Dooley: Hello? Lieutenant Dooley speaking.

(A strange voice responds)

Caller: Well, well, well- if it ain't my old pal Lieutenant 'Bad Ass'
Dooley. Of course, by now, you probably know you're not as
bad as you thought, huh Lieutenant?

Mr. Dooley: Who is this, and what is this all about?... Look, are you
the cowardly scoundrel that hurt my dog and frightened my
kid? Because if you are, when I catch up to you, you are going
to wish that you were never born, you low down son-of-a bi...
(Mr. Dooley is interrupted in his last word.)

Caller: Whoa! Whoa! Hold on there, Lieutenant! Aren't you a family
man, a law abiding, good, upright citizen? Now why would
someone like that be using such foul language? Is it because
they're angry? Or maybe they're scared and don't know what
to do.

Mr. Dooley: You got one of them right, you bastard... I am very angry,
but scared ain't in my vocabulary. However, you are going to
wish that you acquainted yourself with Mr. Scary, because he
probably could have saved you a lot of trouble that you've gotten
yourself into, and anyone else that may be assisting you... I just
want you to know that you all's days are numbered. We will

find you and punish you for all the mess that you think that you have gotten away with.

Caller: Let me tell you something, Lieutenant... I'm not scared of you or any of your little puppets you got running around on a string, trying to find out something that they won't ever find out, unless I want them to. You see, you have no power or authority over me, or anyone connected to me.

I am God; that means I made you, boy... and I can break you whenever I want, so if I were you, I would stop making threats and promises that I can't deliver.

(Mr. Dooley is getting very suspicious of the caller's jargon. It has some similarities to his chief's (Chief McClemens), but he wouldn't dare let the caller on to these suspicions.)

Mr. Dooley: Yeah, you're probably right, caller... So let's say I refrain myself from making threats; what is it that you would want me to do then?

Caller: Now that's my boy! I thought you would never ask until you got your entire family hurt... but it looks like you've wised up just in the nick of time to greet your lovely family, who will be joining you there at the animal hospital shortly. I'll be in touch. *(The caller hangs up)*

**[Mr. Dooley is now very suspicious of the individual on the other end and feels that he has a bigger job ahead than he surmised, especially if the caller is who he suspect them to be.]*

(The Dooley family arrives at the hospital, and the officers escort them into the facility. They ask the receptionist where Mr. Dooley is, and the receptionist points them all to the waiting room. Everyone enters through the door of the waiting room, namely: Mrs. Dooley, Little Jay, Diamerald, Hanna (Dimerald's roomate), Kellie (Mrs. Dooley's sister), Mark (Kellie's son), and Barbara (Sergeant Wllanby's daughter). Both of the accompanying officers stand outside the waiting room. Mrs. Dooley, Little Jay and Diamerald all

walk over to Mr. Dooley and greet him with hugs and kisses. Mr. Dooley tells everyone hello and begins to speak to them...)

Mr. Dooley: I guess all of you are wondering what's going on here, and would like for me to explain why I have you all gathered in protective custody.

Diamerald: (being sarcastic) Now why would we be wondering such a thing, dad? We love having family reunions at the spur of the moment. As a matter of fact, we might even plan another one next week.

(Everybody in the room laughs, including Mr. Dooley)

Mr. Dooley: Okay baby girl, don't they teach you all anything over at that school besides sarcasm?

Mrs. Dooley: (Everyone is still laughing at Diamerald's comedic response to Mr. Dooley) Alright honey, now you lay off my man, he has had a hard day, as we all have…and though we could stand a good laugh, I don't think it's fair for it to be at your dad's expense.

Diamerald: Yeah, you're right mom, I'm sorry dad… but you are to blame. You always taught me to take advantage of opportunities when they present themselves. That was an opportunity to get back at you for the conversation we had earlier, when I was still at school.

(Mr. Dooley and everyone else laughs again)

Mr. Dooley: Okay sweetheart, you got me, and I left myself wide open for that one, but for heaven's sake baby girl, I'm your dad… And boy am
I glad! God help me if I was your enemy. You are pretty good when it comes to being vindictive.

Diamerald: Well, you know what they say daddy, the fruit don't fall too far from the tree, .so you need to be careful about what type of fruit you bare. *(Everybody laughs again)*

Mr. Dooley: Alright, everybody, "Jump on Mr. Dooley Day" is over. Now let's get down to serious business here.

Little Jay: Yeah good, dad, because I want to know when I get to see Alofus.

(*That statement immediately changes everyone's mood of laughter into a more sober mood...*)

Mr. Dooley: Of course, son. Hopefully, the doctor will be out here momentarily, to answer that question and the questions we all have in regards to Alofus' condition.

*{Then Mr. Dooley tells them why they were all brought together in protective custody, so now everyone is knowledgeable of what's going on, to an extent.}

*(Now the doctor (Dr. Smortzen) has just walked in to report the prognosis of Alofus' condition and the extent of the surgery that's about to take place...)

Dr. Smortzen: Well, look-a-here... Are all of you here for the dog named Alofus? *[At one fell swoop, everyone responds,"Yeah, we are."]*
Why doesn't this surprise me? This dog has been some kind of special, ever since he was a puppy... Even my colleagues and I are fans of your dog.

*(Then Mr. Dooley specifies to the doctor that Little Jay is the actual owner, and that he is anxious to know when he can see his best friend.)

Dr. Smortzen: Well hello there, Little Jay, nice to meet the best friend of such a special animal. Did you know how special your dog was, son?

Little Jay: *(not liking the word was, in past tense)* What do you mean was, sir? Does that mean Alofus is dead? Please don't tell me that my dog is dead sir, please! *(Little Jay says all this with hysteria and tears)*

Dr. Smortzen: No... no son, your dog isn't dead, but he is hurt very badly... and that's why I'm here, to let you all know what's going on and what we'll all have to do. *(Mrs. Dooley walks over to Litttle Jay, puts her arms around him, and speaks to Dr. Smortzen.)*

Mrs. Dooley: Whatever you want us to do, Dr. Smortzen, just tell us... we're ready. *(Everyone nods in agreement and mumbles, "Yeah, whatever.")*

Dr. Smortzen: That's great! Well, first and foremost, pray. We need to send up lots of prayers for Alofus and, the other thing is, we are going to have to get some blood for him, he needs a transfusion ASAP... and that's where the difficulty comes in.

Mr. Dooley: And why is that, Dr. Smortzen? What's so difficult?... Just give him the transfusion.

Dr. Smortzen: That's just it, Lieutenant, it's not that simple.

Mrs. Dooley: *(Being a pharmacist herself, she has some medical knowledge.)* Excuse my candor, Dr. Smortzen, and I don't mean to be evasive about your statement, but a blood transfusion shouldn't be that difficult. So what is the real problem here?... And give it to us straight. Okay?

Dr. Smortzen: Okay, you want it straight, but what about the kids here? Are you sure you want me to give it to you straight in front of them?

(Little Jay, Diamerald, Mark, and Hanna all begin to murmur that they are old enough to hear whatever Dr. Smortzen has to say, so Mr. and Mrs. Dooley nod to give the doctor the go-ahead...)

Dr. Smortzen: Okay, then your dog, Alofus... well, not only does he need a blood transfusion, he's also going to need several operations to try and repair the damages that were done to him. Now I don't know how extensive your knowledge is concerning Alofus' injuries, but to better inform you all: in order for him to exist as the dog he once was, or even at all, it's going to take a miracle... and that's putting it mildly.

Mr. Dooley: What type of operations are you referring to, Doc? And please, don't hold back anything.

Dr. Smortzen: He's going to need an eye replacement because the one that was injured is beyond repair. The bones in both of his hind legs are also irreparable, and the extent of trauma to his head is going to require several major operations over a period of months.

Little Jay: Months? What are you talking about, months? I want Alofus to come home now. *(Mrs. Dooley goes to comfort Little Jay again. This time, Barbara assists her.)*

Diamerald: Sounds to me, Dr. Smortzen, that what you are saying is, there really isn't much hope for Alofus.

Dr. Smortzen: Well to put it bluntly, no, not according to medical technology as I know it.

Diamerald: Then maybe we should try it in a way other than what you know, huh Dr. Smortzen?

Mr. Dooley: Now Diamerald, that's no way for you to be talking to Dr. Smortzen, especially when he is trying to help us save Alofus' life.

Diamerald: It don't sound like he's in a position to save his life to me, dad. 'Sounds like Alofus needs a whole new body, a makeover... Yeah... yeah, that's it! I know who can probably help Alofus.

Mr. Dooley: Baby girl, will you please stop all this nonsense?... Who, other than a doctor or God, can help save Alofus? Now please, let Dr. Smortzen finish what he has to say.

Dr. Smortzen: It's okay, Lieutenant, I understand what's going on and its expected of the kids to overreact when they feel that they are about to lose a loved one.

Diamerald: But that's just it, dad and Dr. Smortzen, we don't have to lose Alofus. There is a technology out there that could possibly save his life, or at least give him a fighting chance. I am talking about Bionetic genetism. They have already used it on several human beings to save limbs, eye sight, and even brain damage.

Mr. Dooley: Now baby girl, that's it, I have had enough of this crazy talk! I'm going to have to insist on you keeping quiet here.

Dr. Smortzen: No, hold on a minute, Lieutenant, your daughter just might be on to something. What she is talking about has some validity to it. Where did you hear of this, young lady?

Diamerald: At my school, Jackson State University, where I am studying about Bionics, but if you really want to know more, you will have to talk to my professor, Professor Greer... she's a brilliant woman.

Mr. Dooley: Did you say Professor Greer, sweetheart?

Diamerald: Yes, dad. Why?

Mr. Dooley: Because that's who I visited when I went over to your campus the other day.

Diamerald: Why would you need to visit with Professor Greer, dad? She's not in any trouble or anything, is she?

Mr. Dooley: No, nothing like that, just some police business. Anyhow, I think it would be a good idea for us to give Professor Greer a call. Maybe she can shed some light on a couple of other things for me.

Dr. Smortzen: Whatever we are going to do, in respect to Alofus, it's going to have to be as soon as possible, we don't have much time. How soon can you get hold of this Professor Greer, Lieutenant?

Mr. Dooley: Hopefully right away, Dr. Smortzen. *(Mr. Dooley yells for his officers outside the door to come in. Then he instructs one of them to get over to the school ASAP. Meanwhile, he gets on the phone and calls the university to try and locate Professor Greer.)*

**(Mr. Dooley is on the phone with the receptionist at the laboratory, asking to speak with Professor Greer. Professor Greer has just clicked him on the line, and she is now speaking...)

Prof. Greer: Hello, Professor Greer speaking. How are you doing, Lieutenant Dooley, and how may I help you, sir?

Mr. Dooley: I'm good, Professor, and yourself?

Prof. Greer: I couldn't be better, Lieutenant. Now what has Dr. Elenski done this time?

Mr. Dooley: Excuse me for asking, Professor, but why would you ask me about Dr. Elenski?

Prof. Greer: It was a joke, Lieutenant Dooley... Oh my God, did you take that statement seriously?!

Mr. Dooley: As a matter of fact, Professor, I did, mainly because... even though I am not calling you about Dr. Elenski per say, a few questions about him has pondered my mind. However, I have a more pressing issue at hand that, perhaps, you can help me with.

Prof. Greer: Okay, then let's see. What is it, Lieutenant?

Mr. Dooley: Professor Greer, it is my understanding that you teach a subject that I believe is termed--Bionetics genetism.

Prof. Greer: Yes, Lieutenant, I am teaching that subject. But what is it about that subject that would interest you?

Mr. Dooley: Well Professor, I have a dog, and he has been hurt very badly. The veterinarian here seems to think that repairing him back to good health is hopeless, but my daughter has suggested that we try another alternative... and you are that alternative, Professor Greer.

Prof. Greer: Me?! What could I possibly do for your severely injured dog, Lieutenant? And why would your daughter select me as a candidate or alternate for healing? Who is your daughter and how does she know me?

Mr. Dooley: My daughter, Professor, is Diamerald... Diamerald Dooley. Do you recognize that name?

Prof. Greer: Why yes, of course! Diamerald is your daughter?!... Well, I guess she is, but I would've never known, Lieutenant, although now that you mentioned it, there are a lot of similarities between you two... but that's another story. Anyhow, let's talk this thing over in person, if that's okay with you, sir.

Mr. Dooley: That will be fine. However, I sent a couple of my officers to pick you up and bring you here with us at the M.A.V.A.S.H. I hope that will be okay with you.

Prof. Greer: Well, if you have already ordered them to pick me up, it doesn't look like I have much of a choice, huh Lieutenant? *(They both laugh)*

Mr. Dooley: Okay Professor, I get the point, and thanks... So I guess we will see you shortly then.

Prof. Greer: I suppose so, I am looking forward to meeting Diamerald's family. She's one of my favorite students.
(The professor and Mr. Dooley say goodbye to each other.)

(About twenty minutes later, the professor arrives at the M.A.VA.S.H, being escorted by the officers that Mr. Dooley sent to pick her up. They all enter the facility and Mr. Dooley is now greeting the professor...)

Mr. Dooley: Hello there, Professor Greer, nice seeing you again. Please forgive me for asking you to come to our aid on such short notice. If it was not an emergency, I assure you we would not have bothered you with this.

Prof. Greer: Hello to you too, Lieutenant, and there is no apology needed. After hearing about your dog's accident and that you were Diamerald's dad, I felt compelled to come.

Mr. Dooley: Whatever your reason, Professor, I just want you to know that we are thankful and that your services here want go unrewarded.

Prof. Greer: Wait a minute, Lieutenant Dooley.... No disrespect to you, but I haven't done anything yet and I don't know if I can do anything, but if I can be of assistance, you can count on me to give it my best.

Mr. Dooley: Well, that's all we can ask of you, Professor Greer. The doctor that will oversee the operation, a Dr. Smotzen, should be with us shortly here. Meanwhile, let me take you in to meet with Diamerald and the rest of the family.

Prof. Greer: Great, I was looking forward to that... Lead the way, Lieutenant.

(Now Professor Greer and Mr. Dooley are entering the waiting room, where the family and friends are posted. As soon as Professor Greer enters the room, Diamerald and Hanna recognize her and run over to greet her with a hug. Professor Greer is now speaking...)

Prof. Greer: Hi there you guys! So this is where you all hang out, when cutting class, huh?

Diamerald & Hanna: (both talking simultaneously) Now Professor Greer, you know we don't cut class. You will have (Diamerald)*my mama and daddy
(Hanna)*Mr. and Mrs. Dooley believing that we are cutting class... And even if we were to cut class, it would not be yours; that's our favorite class.

Prof. Greer: Well that's nice to know, young ladies, because you two are my favorites as well. Now who are these two handsome fellows we have here? *(Referring to Little Jay and Mark)*

Diamerald: *(Pointing them out while speaking)* This one here with the big head: that's my little brother, Jonathan. We call him Little Jay, though.... And this one right here is my crazy cousin, Mark, and we call him crazy... I'm just kidding; he doesn't have a nickname.

Prof. Greer: Hello there, guys, how are you all doing?

(Both Little Jay and Mark respond with "Hi! We're okay.")

Diamerald: And this beautiful lady right here, Professor Greer, is my mother. And the one beside her is my lovely Auntie Kellie. She's my mom's sister and also Mark's mom... And last but not least, this is a dear friend of the family, her name is Barbara. Her mom and my dad are co-workers.

(Professor Greer, while looking at all of them, is telling everyone that it's nice to meet such wonderful folks. The doctor, Dr. Smortzen, has just walked into the room. Mr. Dooley is about to introduce him to Professor Greer.)

Mr. Dooley: Hi there, Dr. Smortzen, good to have you back. Guess who else is with us now.

Dr. Smortzen: Let me see here... Now of course, we already had Mrs. Dooley, her sister Kellie, the Beautiful Barbara, the Diabolical Diamerald, the Marvelous Mr. Mark, Hanna Montana in the flesh and the star of the show, Little Jay... so that only leaves this lovely young lady here... And who, may I ask, are you darling?

Prof. Greer: Honey, after referring to me like that and introducing everyone else so eloquently, I will be whoever you want me to be.
(Starts smiling in a flirtatious way.)

(Everyone else quietly oohs as Diamerald and Hanna adds "Professor Greer likes Dr. Smortzen.")

Dr. Smortzen: If that makes her like me then she's in trouble, because there's a lot more of that where that came from... So whoever you are, you better watch out or by the end of the hour, they will be calling you my fiancée. *(Then he and everyone else laughs... everyone except Professor Greer.)*

Prof. Greer: Alright, hold on a sec; I was just trying to be nice. You are not dealing with an amateur here... *(Reaching out her hand to shake his hand, Professor Greer formerly introduces herself to Dr.*

Smortzen.) Hello, how are you? I am Professor Janece Greer, DVM at JSU school of veterinary medicine. Nice to meet you, Dr. Smortzen.

Dr. Smortzen: Likewise, Professor Greer... but you can call me Daryl.

(Talking amongst each other, Diamerald and Hanna says, "Did you see that? She told that man her whole name! In a little while, she will probably be giving him those digits." Then both of them start to sniggle.)

Prof. Greer: Alright girls, I hear you all over there. What's so funny?... Remember the Las Vegas commercial? What happens here stays here. *(When everyone finishes laughing, Mr. Dooley speaks out.)*

Mr. Dooley: Okay, okay; enough of the romance-a-thon. As much as I'd hate to spoil a good thing, we do have more serious business at hand.

Dr. Smortzen: Oh, I'm sorry, Lieutenant. You're right; all jokes aside.

Prof. Greer: Jokes, Dr. Smortzen? You mean to tell me that you were joking when you called me darling? *(Everyone laughs again)*

Dr. Smortzen: No! No way, beautiful! I wouldn't dare joke about a thing like that, my darling clemintine. *(This time everyone laughs even harder.)*

Prof. Greer: Why thank you, honey-pooh! Now we can get on with business.

Dr. Smortzen: Alright, let's not make this a def-comedy jam session. Lieutenant, would you, Mrs. Dooley, and Professor Greer please join me in my office?

(After everyone says their goodbyes, the group that Dr. Smortzen summoned follows him into his office. Once inside, Dr. Smortzen invites Professor Greer and Mr. Dooley to have a seat... He is now speaking to them both.)

Dr. Smortzen: Okay then; now that we have all settled down a bit, we can move forward with our primary objective, which is to try and find common grounds of a solution to repair Alofus' injuries and hopefully save his life. Now, to begin, I would just like to remind you all that, as you already know,   I am only a veterinarian with limited skills so I am not sure if I can be of much help... if any at all. But I'm more than willing to give it my all in whatever I might be capable of here. With that being said, the table is now open for discussion... However, keep in mind that, if Alofus is to have any chance of recovery, time will be a key factor.

Prof. Greer: First off, I would like to tell you, Dr. Smortzen, that you are too kind. And even though you abased yourself rather humbly, your experience has proceeded you in this matter, sir because I, for one, do know that you are one of the best, if not the best, veterinarians in the entire state; perhaps even in the entire country. So to let you all know, Mr. and Mrs. Dooley, your dog Alofus is in very good hands.

Dr. Smortzen: *(With a look of gratitude and blush)* Why thank you, Professor Greer! I really do appreciate such high praises, especially from such an intelligent and beautiful educator as yourself... Please keep talking... *(Everyone laughs)*

(Then Professor Greer continues her speech)

Prof. Greer: Now, if we have all the jokes and flattery aside... *[Everyone laughs again]* On a more sober note, I need to know more about the extent of the dog's injuries so that I can further evaluate what may or may not be needed here.

Dr. Smortzen: Should I, Lieutenant Dooley, or would you care to elaborate a bit here?

Mr. Dooley: No, Dr. Smortzen, all this is out of my league. Please- you go right ahead. Besides, you and Professor Greer seem to be having a good report amongst each other... you know, that connection. *[The laughter resumes.]*

Prof. Greer: Alright now, Lieutenant, I know that you don't want to be charged with a conspiracy here.

Mr. Dooley: What are you talking about, Professor? What on earth would I be conspiring?

Prof. Greer: Conspiring to cause me to lose my singlehood; although it hasn't been all that lately. *[The laughter escalates]*

Dr. Smortzen: Hold on now, Professor, I hope that I haven't been sending the wrong signals... because I never intended to send betrothal signals; I only intended to give a "let's see a movie or eat dinner together" signal... *[The hilarity has climaxed.]*

Mrs. Dooley: Okay everyone; lets settle down here. I thought we left Diamerald, the comedian, down the hall. And Dr. Smortzen, you said that this wasn't a def-comedy jam session, yet you keep on acting like Martin Lawrence or Steve Harvey, whereas Professor Greer is acting like Seymour or that lady who always carries her purse; I believe her name is Sheryl Underwood. As for my lame husband here, God bless his sweet heart, he's acting like a Chris Rock wanna-be... Well, I am about to pull a Russel Simmons on all of you, "God bless you and good night". Now let's move forward with Alofus' business.

Dr. Smortzen: Lieutenant Dooley, where did you find this young lady? Because I'd sho' like to go there and find me one.

(Everyone persists to laugh)

Prof. Greer: Yeah, I'd say she's a keeper. Wouldn't you, Lieutenant?

*(Mr. Dooley gives a look, as if to to say, "If you only knew the other half".)

Mrs. Dooley: Well, I don't know what that's supposed to mean; I'm not exactly Michelle Obama, either.

Mr. Dooley: What, honey? I didn't say anything. Why you trying to diss me?

Mrs. Dooley: Sometimes an expression tells more than words, sweetheart... and I am precise when it comes to reading faces.

{Apart from Mr. Dooley, everyone laughs... Seeing that things are on the verge of getting nasty, Prof. Greer speaks...}

Prof. Greer: Hey, you guys, guess what... The forecasters said that it would be 90 degrees tomorrow, with lots of sunshine.

(Everyone emits one last chuckle and finally settles down.)

Dr. Smortzen: Now what was I saying about Alofus' condition, Professor?... Oh yeah! Well, lets see now... he has two broken hind legs, severe head trauma, the retina in his left eye is destroyed, and he has lost a great deal of blood, which is why he is now being prepped for the transfusion. So what are your thoughts after hearing the diagnosis, Professor Greer?

Prof. Greer: Well, Dr. Smortzen, under normal circumstances, the probability of an animal or even a human recovering from such injuries would be very slim... but I think we have a fighting chance. However, if you all don't mind, I would like to bring another friend and colleague of mine on board for this surgery. It would better our chances of a successful outcome.

Dr. Smortzen: I guess that would be okay, Professor Greer, unless of course, the Lieutenant and his wife objects.

(Both Mr. and Mrs. Dooley concur with the idea, so it is a unanimous decision...)

Dr. Smortzen: If you don't mind me asking, Professor Greer, who is he... this colleague of yours?

Prof. Greer: Well, first of all, Dr. Smortzen, that he is a she. And her name is Dr. Aeilene Kyzar, a doctor of veterinarian prosthetic surgery for large canines. She is a prosthesis specialist. To have her on board with us will increase our chances of a successful revival and revitalization significantly.

Mr. Dooley: Okay, then now that we all are in agreement on what to do, I think it would be judicious for us to get on it ASAP.

Mrs. Dooley: Yeah, I agree. Dr. Smortzen has already intimated how crucial time is.

Dr. Smortzen: Mr. & Mrs. Dooley, no disrespect to you all or the family, but we do have one other obstacle to hurdle here.

Mr. Dooley: And what might that be Dr. Smortzen?

Dr. Smortzen: Lieut. Dooley, I know how emotional this has been thus far for you and your family, and I know how important and meaningful it will be if we can rekindle Alofus' life. However, we all have to face the reality of another aspect of this quest, which is one of the main ingredients of this project. You see, in order for it to be completely possible, without any obstacles, the economic part of it has to be in place. I hope that you all are following me here.

Mrs. Dooley: Yeah, unfortunately, we are Dr. Smortzen. What you are saying is that, even though Alofus is like family, he's not on the family's insurance plan. Correct?

Dr. Smortzen: Well, yes but not exactly, Mrs. Dooley.

Mrs. Dooley: Not exactly?! What else could you be alluding to, Dr. Smortzen?

Dr. Smortzen: What I am trying to say is...

(Prof. Greer interrupts Dr. Smortzen to further explain the economics and politics of the situation...)

Prof. Greer: Please excuse me, Dr. Smortzen, but if you don't mind, allow me to take it from here.

Dr. Smortzen: No, I don't mind Professor... please do.

Prof. Greer: Well, Lieutenant and Mrs. Dooley, first off; I don't know how much knowledge about a procedure of this magnitude you all have, but it definitely isn't easy. However, it could be as easy as one, two, and three after certain steps have been made. We'd have to assemble a great dream team and, as Dr. Smortzen mentioned, economics would play a major part in our efforts to combat the problem at hand. The good news is that I believe that we have accomplished the first step to saving Alofus' life, in that we have Dr. Smortzen here- a renowned veterinarian, myself-a doctor of bionetic genetism, and Dr. Kyzar-who is one of the best, if not the best prosthetic designers and prosthesis doctors in the country. And although we have yet to overcome the economics part, there is an even bigger hurdle for us to leap; that is the hurdle of politics, Mr. and Mrs. Dooley.

Mrs. Dooley: Politics?! Excuse me for sounding presumptuous here Professor, but I don't think politics should be in question for you all to save Alofus' life!

Prof. Greer: Well, Mrs. Dooley, under normal circumstances, you would be absolutely correct... Unfortunately, we are not dealing with a normal circumstance here. You see, we're not just talking about saving Alofus' life; we're talking about practically reinventing him as a robotic animal.

Mr. Dooley: Hold on... Hold on a minute here, Professor Greer!... What did you just say?! I hope it wasn't what I thought I heard. Did you say that Alofus would be a robot?!

Prof. Greer: Well, Lieutenant, not exactly; I said robotic, meaning some of his body parts would be mechanical but not entirely... Anyhow not to discount your conversation, Lieutenant, but it is imperative that we move forward with this because time is definitely of the essence here. So to address Mrs. Dooley's concern about the political factor, since we will be inventing an entirely new creature; neither human nor animal but a mixed breed, if you will, of an animal and a futuristic, robotic creature, we will need approval from the proper authorities on this... and that would be the U.S.D.F.S.R.C. The congress might even have a say in this matter.

Mrs. Dooley: I appreciate your thorough explanation, Professor Greer, and I am understanding your reasoning. However, I would like to know exactly what U.S.D.F.S.R.C stands for.

Prof. Greer: Okay. That is the abbreviation for the United States Department of Futuristic Science Research Center. But as I said, we might still have to get Congress to sign off on this.

Mrs. Dooley: Thanks, Professor Greer, for all of your efforts and explanations to help Mr. Dooley and I further understand this whole process.

Mr. Dooley: Yes, Professor Greer, and I would like to express my gratitude to you and Dr. Smortzen, as well, for your support. Now what is the next step?

Prof. Greer: The next step is for me to E-mail Dr. Kyzar, and to ask her to join Dr. Smortzen and me for a brief meeting. Meanwhile, Lieutenant, you and Mrs. Dooley are free to go and attend to any other personal business that you might need to. I know that you all are probably anxious to get back to your family.

Mr. Dooley: Why yes, thank you! I have some unfinished police business that I would like to get on with.

Dr. Smortzen: Lieutenant, if I may interject to both you and Mrs. Dooley, don't worry yourselves too much about the financial aspect of this, because I know some people who can help.

Mrs. Dooley: Why, thanks again Dr. Smortzen, in advance. Anyhow, we do need to go now honey; let's leave these great people here to get along with their work.

(Everyone in the room says their goodbyes as the Mr. and Mrs. Dooley leaves.)

{Professor Greer has asked for Dr. Smortzen's permission to use his computer and is now accessing the web-site to e-mail Dr. Kyzar, her colleague. Meanwhile, Dr. Smortzen has gone into the other office to make a few phone calls.}

**[Dr. Kyzar is now responding to Prof. Greer's E-mail...]*

Dr. Kyzar's E-mail: Hello, Professor, and how are you doing? I have read your E-mail, although I must admit, I don't fully understand what you are asking of me... but you know, Professor, whatever it is, I am here in support of you. I also see where you stipulated the urgency of the matter and that I should meet with you ASAP over at the M.A.V.A.S.H. Not to despair; I am on my way. See you soon.

{Dr. Smortzen was on the phone with a prominent business associate, trying to convince him to invest in the research type surgery. He has convinced the business associate that, by investing in this project, he would be part owner of perhaps the greatest futuristic invention ever in science research, and that it could prove to be, not only a good political move, but a very lucrative investment as well... so the idea has been sold... Now they are on their phones, with their lawyers working out the legal aspects and specifics of the economics involved in getting the operation under way, which is an estimated three million dollars for the overall surgery and mechanical body

parts, as well as the supervisory and maintenance of the body parts that will be needed for six months to a year once the surgery is completed and rendered a success...}

**(Now Dr. Smortzen is talking to one of the executive directors over at the U.S.D.F.S.R.C. After fully understanding what Dr. Smortzen has set before him, the executive director vows to get back to him with an answer within an hour of meeting with his colleagues. The director stipulates to Dr. Smortzen that even though this is a rather unique situation and a less than normal circumstance, he feels confident in getting them to okay this task; and that, as far as the congressmen are concerned, no bill or law will have to be introduced, because this type of study has already been approved and is under research, although it's primarily only with humans... So now everything has been set in place and the final go-ahead will occur within a couple of hours. The surgery, if approved, will be underway within 3 to 4 hours.)

* [Mr. and Mrs. Dooley have made it back into the waiting area with their other family members and friends. Little Jay and Mark both run up to Mr. Dooley to inquire of the meeting and of Alofus' chances of recovering. Everyone else is now listening as Mr. Dooley responds to Little Jay and Mark.]

Mr. Dooley: Yes, Little Jay and Mark, the meeting appears to have gone well, guys. And Alofus is still holding on. As you all know, he is a real fighter. Dr. Smortzen and Professor Greer have formulated a plan that seems very doable. However, they're going to need some assistance to make this all happen; and by that, I mean they will have to bring in another team mate to help with the prosthetic aspect of it, a Dr. Kyzar. They also have to get an approval from the United States Department of Futuristic Science Research Center. Congress may even need to sign a new bill or law into action.

Diamerald: Is it really that serious, dad?

Mr. Dooley: Unfortunately, honey, it is… Your mom and I felt the same way about the matter until it was further and more thoroughly explained to us.

Little Jay: So what does all this mean in my language, dad?

Mr. Dooley: It means that now Alofus may receive all the help he needs to get well again, son.

Little Jay: Good; that's what I've been waiting to hear. Now I can eat. Mom… dad… can we go get something to eat? I'm starving.

Mrs. Dooley: Sure, son, I am a bit hungry myself.

**(Everyone else murmurs in agreement to being famished. So they all leave the hospital to go out to eat together…)*

{Meanwhile, back at the M.A.V.A.S.H, Professor Greer has gotten in touch with Dr. Kyzar. Dr. Kyzar has agreed to assist her and Dr. Smortzen with the operation; and she is now en route to the hospital. Also, Dr. Smortzen has worked out all the specifics and economics with the U.S.D.F.S.R.C and his prominent business associate, who will invest his money in support of the operation and the advancement of science research.}

**** (Mr. Dooley, along with the rest of the family and friends, are at a diner, helping themselves to a buffet meal. While sitting down at the table to eat, Mr. Dooley gets a call from Corporal Becker (one of his officers who were assisting him and Sergeant Willansby in the Satcher case). Mr. Dooley answers, gets up, and walks from the table to the lobby of the restaurant.)*

Mr. Dooley: Hello, Lieutenant Dooley speaking.

Corp. Becker: Yes, Lieutenant Dooley, this is Corporal Becker, sir. How are you?

Mr. Dooley: Just fine, Corporal Becker, but I am with my family about to have lunch. So how may I be of assistance to you?

Corp. Becker: Oh, I'm sorry for interrupting your lunch; please forgive me. However, I would not be calling if it was not important.

Mr. Dooley: That's quite alright, Corporal. Now what is it that's so important?

Corp. Becker: Well, sir, I think we have a lead on Sgt. Willansby's location.

Mr. Dooley: You do?! That's good news, Corporal. And exactly where would that be; and how did you come about getting that information?

Corp. Becker: From an anonymous caller.

Mr. Dooley: Did you say an anonymous caller, Corporal?

Corp Becker: Yes, that is correct, sir. I was out on patrol and Officer Murtoon called me over the radio from the station headquarters to inform me that an unknown individual was on the phone, wanting to speak with me about Sergeant Willansby's disappearance.

Mr. Dooley: Why you, Corporal? Why would anyone call to speak to you about Sgt. Willansby's disappearance, Corporal?

Corp. Becker: Well, sir, at first I thought the same thing; but when I talked to this anonymous caller, I found out that they somehow knew that you and I were working the case and they said that you were preoccupied with investigating the assault on your son's dog, Lieutenant. How they had knowledge of that is beyond me, sir... But for now, my only concern is if there is any truth to the information about Sgt. Willansby's whereabouts.

Mr. Dooley: I understand Corporal... and I am with you on that issue. Okay, now where is this location, and what is your location right now Corporal?

Corp. Becker: Right now, I am over near the football stadium on Beech Boulevard. And the anonymous caller said that we could find Officer Willansby at an abandoned warehouse over on Moonbeam Avenue. Do you want me to go on over there, sir?

Mr. Dooley: Yes I do, Corporal Becker, but first I want you to call for *plenty* of backup.

Corp. Becker: I'm on it sir.

Mr. Dooley: Becker, on second thought, call for SWAT as well. This could be more dangerous than meets the eye.

Corp. Becker: Alright, Lieutenant. What about you sir?

Mr. Dooley: I am on my way, Corporal Becker, I want you in charge until I get there. I'll see you shortly. Tell everyone that I don't want any actions taken until I get there to assess the situation, Corporal.

Corp. Becker: Yes sir, I got it. *(They both hang up. Mr. Dooley walks back to the table, and is now about to speak to Mrs. Dooley...)*

Mr. Dooley: Honey, I am sorry I ran off like that, but I just got a very important call from one of my men.

Mrs. Dooley: I kind of figured that. Was it good news or bad, sweetheart?

Mr. Dooley: Well, I guess you could say both for now, sweetheart. They have supposedly located Sergeant Willansby.
(Barbara and the others at the table are listening to Mr. Dooley as he speaks to Mrs. Dooley. So Barbara interjects after hearing that statement.)

Barbara: What?! You all found my mom?! That's great! Is she okay?! Where is she, Lieutenant Dooley?!... Is my mom alright?!

Mr. Dooley: Hold on there, Barbara, and please settle down. (For Barbara was getting hysterically upset and a bit loud in the restaurant) I don't know any more than where she is probably located... and I am not even certain of that. So I am going to have to leave you all for now and investigate this alleged location.

Mrs. Dooley: Honey, aren't you going to at least eat your food before you leave?

Mr. Dooley: No, sweetheart, this is very important, as you should know. And as you can see, Barbara is as anxious as I am to see if Sgt. Willansby is okay.

Barbara: Yes I am, Lieutenant, and I would like to come with you.

Mr. Dooley: I know, Barbara. I do understand your concern. However, I can't allow you to come; it may be dangerous... But I promise you that I will call and let you all know as soon as I find out something. Okay?

Barbara: Alright then, Lieutenant. Yes, I do understand your position, sir... And thanks for all your efforts in locating my mom.

Mr. Dooley: You're welcome, Barbara. You are like my own daughter, and your mom is one of my closest friends; so this is very personal.

Mrs. Dooley: Okay, honey, you be careful now and come back to us.

Diamerald: Yeah, dad, please do be careful. I don't know what I would do if something was to happen to you.

Mr. Dooley: Why thanks, baby girl, but you are not going to have to worry about that. Okay, sweetie?

Diamerald: Okay, dad... Love you.

Mr. Dooley: Love you too, baby girl.

Little Jay: I love you too, dad, and hurry back so we can get back over to the hospital to see about Alofus.

Mr. Dooley: Yeah okay, son, I will, but you all will be going back to the hospital without me for now, when everyone finishes eating. I have some other serious unfinished business to attend to.

Kellie: Alright, brother-in-law. You hurry up and come on back here; and do be extra careful. My sister is too young and pretty to be a widow. Besides, you are my favorite brother-in-law.

Mr. Dooley: Thanks, Kellie, that was sweet; but I am your only brother-in-law. *(Everyone laughs)*

(Now, back at the M.A.V.A.S.H, Dr. Kyzar has finally arrived and she is now in a brief meeting with Professor Greer and Dr. Smortzen. They are all getting prepared for Alofus' surgery, which will get underway in about an hour or so.)

**(Also Corp. Becker, along with his back up and the SWAT team, has arrived on the scene of Serg Willansby's alleged location, over on Moonbeam Ave, and they are getting set in position while waiting on Mr. Dooley's arrival, as Corp. Becker was instructed.)*

***(Twenty minutes later, Mr. Dooley arrives at the warehouse on Moonbeam Ave., where Serg. Willansby is allegedly being held. Upon arrival, he is greeted by Corp. Becker with a handshake. Corp. Becker is now speaking to Mr. Dooley...}*

Corp. Becker: Hello, Lieutenant. Good to see you, sir. We have the perimeter secured. The swat team is in position, waiting for your instructions... And, oh yeah, the SWAT team's commander wants to have a word with you.

Mr. Dooley: Thanks for informing me and carrying out my orders as specified, Corporal Becker. Now where is the Swat commander?

Corp. Becker: *(While pointing Mr. Dooley in the direction of the commander)* He is right over there, sir, behind the command mobile unit.

Mr. Dooley: Alright. Just hold your position and I'll get right back with you shortly, Corporal.

Corp. Becker: Will do, sir.

****(*Mr. Dooley is now walking over to meet with the SWAT commander. The SWAT commander notices him approaching and comes out to greet him...)*

Swat Comm.: Hello. How are you doing?... Lieut. Dooley I presume?

Mr. Dooley: Yes... And you are?

Swat Comm: Oh I'm sorry, Lieutenant; I am Captain Valezquez. *(Extending his hand to Mr. Dooley)*

Mr. Dooley: *(Mr. Dooley and the SWAT commander are now shaking hands.)* Nice to finally meet with you, Captain. I've heard quite a bit about you, sir.

Capt. Valezquez: Why yes, of course you have. I hope that it was all good, Lieutenant.

Mr. Dooley: Most certainly, sir. A good officer's work always proceeds him.

Capt. Valezquez: Thanks, Lieutenant. This is true because I have also heard of your good works, and I am glad to be of service to you.

Now what, exactly, would you like for us to do here, Lieutenant Dooley?

Mr. Dooley: Well, sir, I would like for you to take some of your men and go through that abandoned warehouse. Supposedly, one of our own, a Sergeant Willansby, is being held there. She was abducted a couple of days ago, and we just received an anonymous call today, telling us that we could find her inside there.

Capt. Valezquez: Okay, Lieutenant, will do. And by the way, I know Sergeant Willansby. She and I went to the academy together; so for me, this is personal. And we will use extreme caution so that the sergeant is not harmed in this search and siege tactic; you can count on it.

Mr. Dooley: Thanks, Captain, that's nice to know. And I, too, have a personal interest in this matter because ever since I came to the 23rd precinct, Sergeant Willansby and I have been close friends. Now you all can proceed with your orders, sir. And again, do use caution.

(*Capt. Valezquez is ordering the SWAT team to get ready to rush the building, and to be careful to look for wires of booby traps with bombs and/ or other traps.*)

[*Mr. Dooley walks back over to Corp. Becker and orders him and the back up officers to get in a ready position. While talking to Corp. Becker, Mr. Dooley receives a call from the chief of police, Chief McClemens. Mr. Dooley is now answering his phone...*]

Mr. Dooley: Hello, Lieutenant Dooley here.

Chief McClem: Yeah, I know who you are, Lieut. Dooley, and I am Chief McClemens, chief of the Jackson Police Department, wherein you are employed. That makes me your chief as well,

Lieutenant. So why do you feel you can go around giving orders to SWAT without my authorization?

Mr. Dooley: Excuse me sir, and no disrespect to you, but...*(Chief McClemens cuts him off)*

Chief McClem: But nothing, Lieut. Dooley, and you have disrespected me. Didn't I tell you to keep me posted on this matter?

Mr. Dooley: Why, yes sir, you did... But I guess I overreacted when I heard that Sergeant Willansby had possibly been located.
Maybe I should have taken out the time to inform you of the progress of the investigation, sir. I am sorry; it wasn't intentional... But right now, I have a serious task that I am in the middle of, sir, so I'll give you a call when it's completed. *(Mr. Dooley hangs up the phone.)*

Chief McClem: No, you don't have a task to... Hello?... Hello?... Lieutenant Dooley, are you there? Hello?... Now I know he did not just hang up on me.
(Meanwhile, Mr. Dooley decides not to concern himself, at this point, with the chief's power pull for fear that it would possibly compromise his efforts to rescue Serg. Willansby. So he continues the mission at hand and orders the SWAT team to go ahead and storm the warehouse... And SWAT does just that, searching and seeking throughout the facility without any opposition because no one was in the building... so they thought... until one of the SWAT officers suddenly yelled out, "Here; she's over here, sir." - referring to Serg Willansby. Now that she has been located, the SWAT commander, Capt. Valezquez, has been informed and is now on his two-way, calling Mr. Dooley to inform him of the news...)

Capt. Valezquez: *{using radio communication}* Captain Valezquez to Lieut. Dooley; the cat has located the mouse... Repeat... the cat has located the mouse.

Mr. Dooley: *{responding in radio communication}* Copy that, Captain Valezquez, the homeowner is on the move. See you in two.

Capt. Valezquez: Roger that... Over and out.

*{*Mr. Dooley and Corporal Becker are now on their way to see what condition Serg. Willansby is in... They are now entering the room, where SWAT officers are attending to Serg. Willansby. She is conscious but very weak from dehydration and fatigue. Although she is still tied up, the tape has been removed from her mouth and she is trying to speak, as Mr. Dooley walks in. He hurries to her aid, kneels down to her side, and cradles her head onto his lap. Then he begins to speak to her briefly...*}

Mr. Dooley: *(while rubbing Serg. willansby's head, as she looks up at him with a mixed look of thankfulness and dehydration)* Get me some water here, ASAP, Corporal Becker. And do we have an ambulance on the way?

Capt Valezquez: Yes, Lieutenant, I've already called them. They should be here any minute now.

**(*Corporal Becker hands Mr. Dooley the water. Then Mr. Dooley gradually pours small portions into her mouth, while holding her head up. He then pours some water into his hand and rubs it across her forehead. He tells her to hold on, and not to try to speak. He lets her know that an ambulance is on the way, and he asks for some assistance to carry her outside. By the time they get outside, the ambulance pulls up. She is put into the ambulance and taken to the hospital, while Mr. Dooley follows in pursuit...*}

(While following close in behind the ambulance, Mr. Dooley calls Mrs. Dooley and the family to inform them of the good news about Serg. Willansby...)

Mrs. Dooley: Hello, honey, how are things going?

Mr. Dooley: They're going well, sweetheart. We did find Sergeant Willansby.

Mrs. Dooley:*(Screaming in immediate excitement)* You did?! You really found her?! Oh my God, ya'll, they found Sergeant Willansby!

(At that moment, Barbara, Sergt Willansby's daughter, snatches the phone away from Mrs. Dooley. She is now speaking to Mr. Dooley...)

Barbara: Hello? Hello? Lieutenant Dooley, did you all really find my mom? Is she alright?... Please tell me that she's okay; please.

Mr. Dooley: Okay, okay, sweetie; just calm down and I'll tell you. Please settle down, Barbara. We don't need you getting sick here. Alright?

Barbara: Alright, alright; I'm settled, Lieutenant. Please just tell me whether or not my mom is okay before I lose my mind.

Mr. Dooley: Yes, Barbara, your mom is okay. She's just a little dehydrated; that's all... but she will be alright.

Barbara: Where is she? I want to see her, Lieutenant. Where's my mom?

Mr. Dooley: Well, right now she is in the ambulance, on her way to the hospital; and I am following behind. We are on our way to St. Mary's Memorial Hospital.

Barbara: Okay. Thanks, Lieutenant Dooley, I am on my way.

Mr. Dooley: Wait a minute, Barbara, you can't just run out like that. Give me a couple of minutes and I will radio an officer and have him bring you over to the hospital. Alright, dear? Please, just do that much for me... and I promise you, I will get you to your mom as soon as possible. Alright?

Barbara: Okay, Lieutenant Dooley, I'll be waiting... Just hurry up!

Mr. Dooley: I will, sweetheart. I know how much you love your mom and are anxious to reunite with her, so I'll see you soon.

**(Mr. Dooley says goodbye and hangs up. He is now getting another phone call. Mr. Dooley answers the phone...)

Mr. Dooley: Hello, Lieutenant Dooley speaking. Who's calling?

Caller: Hello, Lieutenant Dooley, this is Dr. Smortzen with M.A.V.A.S.H. How are you doing?

Mr. Dooley: Oh yeah... sorry I didn't recognize your voice. Hello Dr. Smortzen. I'm fine, and how are you?

Dr. Smortzen: Just fine, Lieutenant. Now to get down to the purpose of this call... Well, Lieutenant, I was calling you to inform you that Professor Greer and I have gotten everything in place and are ready to go forward with the surgery. Also, Professor Greer's colleague, Dr. Kyzar, has come aboard to assist in the operation... And as for the economic and political constituents... well, they have been worked out. So don't worry yourself with those issues. Okay? And if it's okay with you and the family, sir, we would like to commence with the operation immediately.

Mr. Dooley: Why thank you, Dr. Smortzen, for all your efforts and please convey my sentiments to Professor Greer and her colleague for me as well. But you know that we're excited about you all getting started here so, by all means, please do. Meanwhile, I will contact the wife and family and have them get on back over there right away, but I won't be joining you all for a while; I have some other pressing business at hand. Again, thanks, Dr. Smortzen... and I will be praying with you all. Goodbye.

**{Mr. Dooley hangs up. He has already instructed an officer to take Barbara over to St. Mary's Hospital, where Serg. Willansby was taken for treatment. Now he is ordering the other officers to escort the rest of the family back to M.A.V.A.S.H. He's about to arrive at St. Mary's Hospital... Mr. Dooley is now getting out of his car and is headed toward the entrance of the emergency room, where the Emt's have just taken Serg. Willansby.

Now inside, he is walking up to one of the emergency room doctors to introduce himself...}

Mr. Dooley: *[Pulls out his badge and flashes his I.D. to the doctor]* Hello, I am Lieut. Dooley with the Jackson Police Department, and this is one of ours (pointing to Serg. Willansby). She was abducted a couple of days ago. We just rescued her, so please give her your undivided attention and the best care you got, Doc.

Doctor: Hello, nice to meet you, Lieut. Dooley. I am Dr. Latrell and I am sorry about your Sgt. But, of course, we will attend to her with the best care, Lieutenant, as we do with all our patients. Now you can have a seat over there in the waiting room, sir. We will take it from here.

(Mr. Dooley, taking note of the doctor's innuendoes, goes over to the waiting area and sits down.)

**{Barbara, Sergt Willansby's daughter, is being escorted down the hall. Mr. Dooley has just spotted her, so he gets up to greet her...}*

Mr. Dooley: Hello, Barbara, good to see you... Come on into the waiting area here with me and I will fill you in on your mom's condition.

Barbara: Okay, Lieut. Dooley, that sounds good.

(Mr. Dooley and Barbara both sit down in the waiting room.)

Mr. Dooley: Alright, Barbara, I know that you are anxious to see your mom... and you will get to see her in a little while... but for now the doctor is trying to stabilize her. She was very dehydrated and had a few minor cuts and bruises. However, there's nothing to worry about. Barbara, your mom is a strong and courageous woman. She will be alright. We found her in an abandoned warehouse over on the southside.

Barbara: How is my mom's spirit, Lieut. Dooley, and how on earth were you all able to find her?

Mr. Dooley: Your mom's spirit is good, or at least as well as to be expected under the circumstances, Barbara. And believe it or not, we were tipped off by an anonymous caller over the phone as to where we would possibly find her. Fortunately for us and your mom, the caller was telling the truth. Although the mystery still remains as to who we got the call from and why, we are working just as hard to find out who is behind all this. And I assure you Barbara, sweetheart, that we will find out who did this to your mom.

Barbara: Thanks for finding my mom, Lieut. Dooley, and I am glad she is okay. Thanks be to God for watching over her. And thank you for wanting to find her abductors, Lieutenant, but maybe we should leave well enough alone. Afterall, she made it back safely. Maybe that is a sign for you and my mom to leave that other case you all are working on alone as well... you know, that uh... Satcher case.

Mr. Dooley: And you are very welcome, Barbara, but as far as giving up on the perpetrators who abducted your mom, I am sorry... We can't let them get away with kidnapping a police officer or making threats. I know that you mean well, little darling, but this is serious police business; we will handle it as such. And I don't mean to seem unconcerned about your mom, either, but I gotta get back over to M.A.V.A.S.H. to see about Alofus or Little Jay and Diamerald will never forgive me. But I promise you, I will be back as soon as possible, sweetie. So I need you to hold down the fort here; do it for your mom. Alright, love?

Barbara: Okay, Lieut. Dooley, I understand. Please don't worry about us... and tell Little Jay and the family we are praying for Alofus.

Mr. Dooley: Yes, Barbara, I will be sure to tell them.

Barbara: And you be careful, sir. Even though my real dad died years ago, if something were to happen to you, it would be like déjà vu. What I am trying to say is, I love you like a father, sir.

Mr. Dooley: Thanks, Barbara, that is so sweet of you to say. I will be careful, darling, and you are like a daughter to me too. Now I gotta go, but the officer here will remain with you and your mom. I will be in touch if you all need me for anything. Okay?

Barbara: Okay, Lieutenant. Goodbye.

**(Mr. Dooley has left the hospital and is on his way over to the M.A.V.A.S.H., where his family is sitting in the waiting room as Alofus gets operated on.}

*(Mr. Dooley has made it back to the hospital and he is now walking into the waiting room...)

Little Jay: [Runs over to his dad to greet him at the door] Hi, dad! Boy am I glad you're here! Guess what... Dr. Smortzen and Professor Greer are down the hall operating on Alofus this very minute. Aren't you happy for him, dad? Alofus is going to be well. Then he will be able to catch the frisbee with his mouth again when Mark and I throw it to him.

Mr. Dooley: Yeah, son, I am very happy to know that Alofus is going to get well, and that you and your cousin, Mark, will be able to play all sorts of games with him again... But I don't want you to be getting too excited just yet, Little Jay, because even if Alofus makes it through the surgery, I am sure it's going to be a while before he can play with you guys. Okay?

Little Jay: What do you mean when you say a while, dad?... A week?... Two weeks?... I hope it won't take any longer than that.

Mr. Dooley: Son, it's really....

(Mrs. Dooley asks Mr. Dooley to let her explain it to Little Jay. For she feels that she will be more considerate of Little Jay's feelings than he will be while conveying the prognosis of Alofus' possible recovery.)

Mrs. Dooley: Little Jay, sweetie, what your dad is trying to tell you is that we are not yet sure how Alofus is going to feel about playing so soon. After going through everything that he has gone through, he might want to rest for a while... you know... he might not feel like he can trust anybody just yet. So we don't want to rush him. We should allow him to take his time. And when he is ready, he will let us know, son. Remember, Little Jay, you said it yourself... Alofus is a smart dog.

Little Jay: I guess you are right, mom; Alofus is a smart dog, so Mark and I will just have to wait until Alofus is ready then. But I know when he sees us, it won't take him very long to decide.

Mrs. Dooley: Let's hope that you are right, son.

(Now Diamerald is speaking to dad)
Diamerald: Dad, are you going to tell him?

Mr. Dooley: Tell who what, Diamerald?

Diamerald: Tell Little Jay the truth about Alofus. I think he needs to know before he sees him, dad.

Mr. Dooley: Know what, baby girl? What exactly are you talking about, Diamerald?

Diamerald: I am talking about you all telling Little Jay the truth about Alofus, dad; that even if he survives the surgery, he won't be the same dog. Let him know that Alofus will be part robot. I think that we should tell him, mom and dad, so that he won't be in a state of shock when he first sees his dog again.

Mr. Dooley: No, Diamerald, I don't think it would be appropriate for you nor your mom or I to discuss that sort of thing with Little Jay, especially when we, ourselves, are not that knowledgeable about this bionic development; and even though you are studyng about it, neither are you. So please, let's leave this to the doctors, baby girl. Okay?

Diamerald: Well, I guess so...

Mrs. Dooley: No, we are not asking you to guess whether or not you are going to try to explain this to Little Jay, Diamerald. We explicitly forbid you to. Now is that understood?

Diamerald: Yes, ma'am... it's understood.

Mrs. Dooley: Good, then we are through with that conversation.

** *{Mr. Dooley is glad that Mrs. Dooley stepped in and persuaded Diamerald to leave that conversation to the professionals. Now the receptionist has just come into the waiting room to speak to the Dooley family on behalf of Dr. Smotzen...}*

Recept: Hello, Lieutenant, Mrs. Dooley, and to the rest of your family. I would like to have a brief word with you all.

(Everyone gathers around and takes their seats, as to give the receptionist their undivided attention.)
[Mr. Dooley, speaks to the receptionist...]

Mr. Dooley: Ma'am, if this brief word with us is to express some negative circumstances surrounding the surgery of our dog, then I would prefer the kids not to be included in this meeting. Just tell me and Mrs. Dooley, and we will handle the rest.

Recept: I understand, Lieutenant, but it's not anything negative, sir. However, it is about your dog. Dr. Smortzen just wanted me to let you all know that the surgery went well and that your dog,

Alofus, is in the recovery room, where he will be for about 4 to 6 hours before they will know whether or not the surgery was a complete success. He also wanted me to tell you that that he would be out in about an hour to speak with you all in person, along with Professor Greer and Dr. Kyzar. He says to continue to pray, because your dog is not out of the woods yet, so to speak... but he has survived the first step.

Mr. Dooley: Why, thank you for that good news, ma'am, and you can tell him we will do just that.

Little Jay: (Looking puzzled) So dad, if the surgery went well, then why is the lady asking us to keep on praying for Alofus?... And what is this about him being out in the woods, dad? I don't get it.

Mr. Dooley: Well, son, the lady didn't mean that Alofus was literally in the woods... What she meant is that, in other words, when someone or something is hurt, sometimes they feel like they are in another place... like the woods for instance... and when they get better, they come out of those woods. That's why she said he was not out of the woods yet, and that is why we should keep praying; so that Alofus will come out of the woods. Get it?

Little Jay: Yeah, dad, I got it this time.

Diamerald: Oh my God! Can you believe it, Hanna and Mark?! Little Jay actually got it without having to repeat it over and over.

(Hanna and Mark both laugh. Then Mrs. Dooley speaks...)

Mrs. Dooley: Honey, now that's not nice. Give your brother more credit than that.

Diamerald: But I was giving him credit, mom. I didn't mean it in a negative way at all.

Mrs. Dooley: Really?! You, Diamerald, were praising your little brother? I find that hard to believe... but I'll take your word for it this time.

(*Then Little Jay speaks out again*)
Little Jay: So what are we all waiting for? Mom dad... everybody... let's get started.

Diamerald: Boy, what are you talking about now?

Mr: Dooley Alright, baby girl, leave your little brother alone. Okay?

Diamerald: Oh, alright, dad... Okay, Little Jay, what is it that you want for us to do then?

Little Jay: Pray... The lady said that we should continue praying for Alofus and I want to lead the prayer for him.

Mr. Dooley: Good, Little Jay, that will be wonderful. Please do; go ahead and lead us in prayer, son.

Mrs. Dooley: Yeah, Little Jay, that is a good idea, honey. Now everybody, let's bow our heads and join hands while Little Jay says a prayer for Alofus.
(*Everyone bows their heads and joins hands.*)
(*Diamerald, Hanna and Mark are smiling and smirking. Mrs. Dooley shushes them to stop it.*)

Little Jay: Our Father, God, I don't know you but I am sure you know me; and I don't know where you are, but they tell me you are in heaven. I don't know where that is either, but I bet my dad does; he knows where every place is. He's a cop... but I guess you know that already. They tell me you know everything, God, so I'm not going to bother to tell you my name because you probably already know it. But I would like to ask you for your help since you know everything. And you know your way around on this earth; I know you do God because they told me

you made it in seven days. Boy was that quick! Honestly, I don't
know how you did it; but since my mom, my dad and even my
Sunday school teacher, Mr. Patrolie, told me you did... well, I
guess it's true. Anyhow, I have a dog and his name is Alofus.
You probably already knew that, too. However, he was hurt by
some bad men a few days ago and now they tell me he is out
there in some woods. Well, since you know your way around
this earth, with all these woods you created, I was wondering
if you could help him find his way out, because Alofus is a
good dog, God, and he was hurt once before as a puppy. So
you know that he has suffered enough already. If you don't
know it, then you can ask my NaNa and Paw Paw; they saw
it before they left to go and be with you, God... up there in
heaven. And I don't know if they see the news or not up there,
about what's going on down here on earth, but just in case they
don't know, will you please tell them something for me? Tell
them that Alofus has grown to be a big, smart dog and that he
is even able to catch a frisbee with his mouth... Oh and yeah...
tell them that he even knows how to dial 911... Please, God, if
you do this for me, I promise you I will always be grateful to
you; to do everything you ask of me, except stop eating sweets
because I love candy, cakes, cookies, and ice-cream; they are my
favorites... That's all for now, God. Amen.

(*Everyone else says Amen simultaneously*)

{*Then Mrs. Dooley, Diamerald, Kellie, and Hanna all go over to Little Jay
to hug him and praise him for doing such a good job with the prayer for
Alofus.*}

(*Mr. Dooley is now speaking to Little Jay...*)

Mr. Dooley: Little Jay, that was the best prayer I ever heard, son, and
I am very proud of you.

Mrs. Dooley: It sure was, son... and not only did God hear it, but I bet Alofus heard it, too, and he is on his way out of those woods right now.

Little Jay: Really?! Do you think so mom?!

Mrs. Dooley: Yes, I do Little Jay. Just you wait and see; it won't be long.

Little Jay: You hear that, Mark and Diamerald? Mom said that Alofus and God heard me, and now Alofus will be on his way out of the woods soon.

Diamerald: Yeah, I heard it, little brother, and I believe it, too, because you did do a great job on asking God to help Alofus find his way out of the woods.

Mark: Yeah, cousin Jay, I heard it... and I'll be waiting with you for Alofus to come out of the woods. Okay, Little Jay?

Kellie: And I, too, am very impressed with your prayer to God, Little Jay. I know that God did hear you. Sometimes it's not what we ask God for; it's how we ask him... and you gave God the praises that he is worthy of Little Jay... I know he wouldn't dare turn you down after the way you called on him. You know, Little Jay, God loves it when we trust in him and lean not to our own understanding. He really would like for us to always do this but, of course, we don't. Nonetheless, you let God know, Little Jay, that even though he already knew, you still wanted to talk to him. This should be a lesson to all of us here.

** (*Everyone nods in agreement, signifying that it was touching and uplifting to them as well.*)

* {*Now in about five minutes, Dr. Smortzen, Professor Greer, and Dr. Kyzar will join the Dooleys and Hanna in the waiting room.*}

[Dr. Smortzen, Professor Greer and Dr. Kyzar has just walked into the waiting room. Mr. Dooley and Little Jay greets them all. Little Jay speaks first....]

(As they enter the door, Little Jay *runs over to the three doctors excitedly and anxiously. He hopes that they have some good news about Alofus.*)

Little Jay: Hello, Dr. Smortzen, Professor, and... who are you? *(Referring to Dr. Kyzar who he never got acquainted with)*

Dr. Kyzar: Why, hello there, little handsome fellow. I am Dr. Kyzar, a friend and colleague of Professor Greer here... and who are you?

Little Jay: Me? Oh, I'm Little Jay, and Alofus is my dog. So, Dr. Smortzen, is the operation all done yet? Is Alofus out of the woods?

Dr. Smortzen: Um... what a smart young man you are, Little Jay! What do you know about the term getting out of the woods?

Little Jay: Not much... All I know is when somebody is hurt, it means they went into the woods and if they want to feel better, they have to come out; that's all.

Dr. Smortzen: Well, that's sort of right, Little Jay, but that's not the entire story.

Little Jay: Really? Well, what more is there, Dr. Smortzen? Because if there is more, then mom and dad either forgot to finish the story or didn't know how.

Dr. Smortzen: No, I doubt that Little Jay. I am sure mom and dad knows the rest of the story. Perhaps they just wanted me to tell you the rest.

Little Jay: Oh yeah... now I am remembering... Come to think of it, dad did tell Diamerald that he wanted to leave something to the professionals. I suppose he was referring to you guys.

Dr. Smortzen: Yes, of course he was... And now to finish the story for you... I am going to ask Professor Greer, if she doesn't mind, to finish telling you the story about being hurt and coming out of the woods. So, if you would, Professor Greer, please explain the conclusion of this story to Little Jay for us.

Prof. Greer: Why sure; I'd love too... Okay; then let's see now... How should I start this?... Oh yeah; I know... Well, Little Jay, you see, when someone, or something in this case, gets hurt and is lost in the woods, even though they might want to come out of the woods right away, it's not that easy. You see, because the woods are filled with lots of trees and forests that all look so much alike, it's very difficult for one to find their way out without someone's help. For instance, even in the city, we need the GPS navigation system to help us locate certain places. Even though we are living in the city, we need other assistance to help guide us through and, in the woods, the GPS system is like the doctor to us. So we have to cut down some of the trees and forests so that someone can find their way out easier. And that is what we have done for your dog, Alofus, Little Jay. So now we are all just waiting to see how smart Alofus really is. We have to see if he will be able to find his way out now that we have cut down a few trees and pointed him in the right direction. Do you understand what I am saying, Little Jay?

Little Jay: Yes, ma'am. As a matter fact, I think I do... but I'm not worried now, because Alofus is a very smart dog. I know that he is going to find his way out of those woods.

Prof. Greer: Yeah, Little Jay, that's exactly it. 'Looks like Alofus is not the only smart one here... Okay, now the floor will be momentarily open for discussion and Q's and A's. Now who wants to go first? *[Because Diamerald has been boiling with anticipation to* *have someone explain to Little Jay that Alofus is not going to be the same, she quickly replies to Professor Greer, "Me! Me! Professor Greer, I want to go first!"...]*

Diamerald: Okay, Professor Greer, what I would like to know, from whomever has the answer, is now that the operation is completed, and if everything else goes well, exactly what will Alofus be like? I mean, like, will he be the same or what?

Prof. Greer: Well, first off, I would just like to tell you that that is a very pertinent question, Diamerald. However, if it's okay with you and my colleague here, Dr. Kyzar, I would like to pass this question on to her to answer. Dr. Kyzar, if you don't mind, please...

Dr. Kyzar: Why yes, Professor Greer, I am delighted to entertain that question, young lady. Oh, I am sorry... I mean Diamerald... Is that correct? Diamerald is your name. Is it not?

Diamerald: Yes, ma'am, that is correct.

Dr. Kyzar: Okay, I am going to try and answer your question bluntly... No, your dog, Alofus, will not be the same per say. Of course, he will keep some of his old characteristics, but from a physical and mental stand point, he will be more than a normal specie. What I am trying to say here, Diamerald, to you and to the rest of the family is that, considering that everything goes well and he finds his way out of the woods as we have all concluded, Alofus will no longer be an ordinary dog, but a rather extraordinary one. What I mean when I say extraordinary, Diamerald, is that... for instance, an ordinary dog already hears ten times better than us humans, but Alofus will be able to hear better than an ordinary dog. He will be able to hear up to a half a mile away. A well trained dog can learn about fifteen commands. With this technology, Alofus will be able to learn 150 commands, ten times your average dog. As one scholar once said, dogs not only inhabit our homes, but our hearts, with their never ending loyalty, comic behavior, vibrant personalities, and heroic deeds. Though dogs are our companions, they can also become our closest friends and dearest confidants. They think more like humans than any other animal... yes, even the chimpanzee. Social intelligence is extraordinary. For dogs are bilingual, learning to communicate to humans and their counter parts. They can also distinguish objects by name. Dogs and wolves are genetically 99.8% the same specie, yet it is impossible to turn a wolf into a dog, no matter how much training and love you give it. Nevertheless, Alofus will now have a wolflike instinct, which is why this sort of surgery was not an option, but was very necessary if Alofus was to have any chance at an ordinary life again. Thankfully, he will have that chance. However, it is an extraordinary opportunity of a lifetime, which even a human would welcome; the chance to become an ambassador, if you will, for a new kind of creature with animal, robotic, bionic, and supernatural qualities. Alofus will now be a super dog, a pioneer in the science world of animal research. We enhanced his left eye with a new, more advanced retina. It now has the capability of infrared technology, which will allow him to see, not only during the daylight hours but at night, as far away as 900 feet. For those of you who don't grasp it, that's 300 yards up close and personal, which is three times the length of a football field. His brain and hind legs, which had all been damaged, will now have blue-tooth technology, helping him to know how to move. The implants are fitted around the nerves of his spinal canal. They are connected to a power unit that picks up the signal coming down from the brain. The wires boost the power under the skin to stimulate the muscles. This is a new technology called intraosseous. To operate it, we attach an implant made of titanium alloy to the main bone of the legs, which allows the dog's skin to grow into the metal, making it more like a limb and enabling him to jump as high as a 10 foot fence or wall. You see, Alofus' legs were so torn up that we were not able to repair them, so he is now an amputee... An amputee generally gets prosthetic replacements, and they would normally have to will their prosthetics to make every movement. However, even though the limbs are gone, that does not mean that the remaining nerves have stopped working. This is where Professor Greer and I come in. We have given Alofus a bionic spine and have replaced his natural bones with a joint made of cobalt chrome and polyurethyene. Due to the beating he endured from the perpetrators, the herniated disc in his back was dislocated which, in turn, has disabled both of his hind legs and he has no feeling in them. So we inserted two bolts in the center of his spine to fuse the vertebrae where the spine was crushed. The nerves are inside the spinal cord and the bolts relieve the pressure on it. Because the bolts push the vertebrae apart and relieve the sciatic nerve, this will help the spinal cord to start operating properly again. And since the damage to the cord is not permanent, then Alofus will be just fine. However, he will have to undergo four sessions of physiotherapy and hydrotherapy a day to build up the muscles in his hind legs. This will enable Alofus to, not only run again, but run faster and cut or twist. As a matter of fact, Alofus will be able to outrun any animal in the world at 90 miles per hour, surpassing even the greyhound dog, the leopard tiger, and... yes, even the cheetah. A normal human being or even a super athlete would not stand a chance... and his strength will be mind boggling! We have connected one of the most advanced jaw bones and teeth apparatuses known in the technological world of science, making it strong enough to bite through a rubber tire with ease. This is not just a replacement, people, but an improvement and a step forward for artificial research as we know it. And just in case you all are wondering if Alofus is being used here as some sort of canine research experiment, that is not the case. For there has been at least eleven other dogs that have had, at one time or another, some sort of implant- be it a paw, leg, or jaw bone replacement- but none of them were to the extent that Alofus is undergoing here, and definitely not in the economical neighborhood when you factor in the entire cost overall. His is probably more expensive than the other eleven surgeries combined. If everything goes as we anticipate, your dog Alofus will even be superior to all those other dogs.

And though this may sound like science fiction, it isn't. This is very mainstream medicine. We have been researching this for a long time and it is a proven development in veterinary medicine. This procedure gives Alofus what Mother Nature intended for all dogs to have, a biomechanically sound ball-and-socket joint. And with the combination of modern veterinary thinking and modern materials, this makes it possible to replace many canine body parts, from tattooing pigment on a dog's nose to implanting titanium alloy in its hind legs. Nonetheless, with all this said Little Jay, Alofus is not yet out of the woods. I am sure that for the family having to see Alofus here, severely injured, was a heart wrenching experience. So when you all see him in this new form, it will probably be another heart wrenching experience... only on a more positive note. So, Diamerald, I hope that I have answered your questions to satisfactory, my dear.

Diamerald: Have you?! Boy, did you ever! You probably have answered everybody else's questions, too. *(Everyone laughs)*

Prof. Greer: I'm sorry, Dr. Kyzar, you have to excuse my student, Ms. Diamerald. She generally has a way with words.

Dr. Kyzar: Oh, that's quite alright professor; I'm rather impressed. I see that she and Little Jay here are truly siblings... probably rivalry siblings, huh Diamerald?

Diamerald: You got it, Doc... You are pretty smart yourself.

Dr. Kyzar: Why, thank you Diamerald! Your mom and dad have got to be very proud of you, too.

Mrs. Dooley: Yes. As a matter of fact, we are, Dr. Kyzar... but sometimes we would like to make a swap. *(Everyone laughs)*

Diamerald: Alright, mom, don't make me pull a rabbit out of the hat on you.

Mrs. Dooley: Yeah, you just try it Houdini! Remember, the clay is never smarter than the potter, so I wouldn't try it if I were you... You might not like it if mom pulls a Houdini of her own, and makes rabbit stew out of that rabbit.

[Mark, Little Jay, and Diamerald's room mate, Hanna, all laugh really loudly]

Mr. Dooley: Honey... baby girl... take it from your dad; that's one bunny you won't find funny. Put it back in the hat while you still can.

Diamerald: Yeah, you are absolutely right, dad. I better leave it alone because fruit don't fall too far from the tree... and I smell a rotten apple brewing here.

Mrs. Dooley: You're probably right, dear... an apple full of worms... so, for your sake, I wouldn't bite it.

Hanna: Diamerald, you my girl and all, but I think it's time for you to hold up the white flag, Boo.

Mark: Yeah, Diamerald, you are no match for Auntie Dooley; she's my mom's sister, remember?

Diamerald: Okay, okay everybody, I get it. Alright, mom, you may have won this battle, but the war ain't over, sweetie.

Mrs. Dooley: That's fine with me, baby girl... They told me it's possible that Clint Eastwood and I are kinfolks.

Diamerald: How is that, mom?

Mrs. Dooley: For me to be challenged, "It makes my day."

(Everyone laughs and Diamerald surrenders to the conversation)

[Professor Greer is now speaking...]

Prof. Greer: Well, it looks like we are through with the Q's and A's so, if its okay with you all, we gotta get back to some unfinished business.

Mr. Dooley: Hold on a minute, Professor... Actually, I do have one other question for you all.

Prof. Greer: Yeah sure, go ahead, Lieutenant. What is it?

Mr. Dooley: What I want to know, and I am sure Little Jay and everyone else would like to know too is, how long will Alofus be in recovery?... And how soon can we expect him, if at all, to be able to, perhaps, fetch a frisbee, Professor?

Prof. Greer: That's a good question as well, Lieutenant. But you mean to tell me that after that 30 minute seminar my colleague, Dr. Kyzar, just gave us, she didn't cover that issue? *{Everyone laughs}*

Mr. Dooley: I don't know, Professor... I guess she didn't. It is possible that, when she was explaining the extraordinary features, that I got so caught up in all the excitement and missed that part.

Dr. Kyzar: Alright, you all, get off Dr. Kyzar... This ain't "Beat up on Dr. Kyzar Day". Okay?

Prof. Greer: Alright, let's not get testy here, young lady. *(The laughing persists, then Prof. Greer proceeds to answer Mr. Dooley's question...)* Okay, now back to your question, Lieutenant... Alofus will be out of recovery within the next three to four hours; and as for him chasing a frisbee... we will have to wait and see. We will continue to run tests and evaluate Alofus' routine performance and systematic progression on a daily basis... I hope that answer is sufficient, because we really must be going now.

Mr. Dooley: Yes, Professor Greer, that answer does suffice me... And I, too, need to finish some business.

[Everyone says their goodbyes. Then the 3 surgeons and Mr. Dooley leave the waiting room. He is now calling Barbara, Serg. Willansby's daughter, to ask her about the prognosis of her mom's condition. Barbara is now answering the phone....]

Barbara: Hello, Barbara speaking.

Mr. Dooley: Hi, Barbara, Lieut. Dooley here. How are things going with your mom?

Barbara: Everything is just fine, Lieutenant. As a matter of fact, I just came out of her room a moment ago and she seemed to have a good spirit.

Mr. Dooley: That is good news, Barbara, and I am glad to hear that your mom has a good spirit after such a traumatic experience. I told you that she was a fighter. Didn't I?

Barbara: As a matter of fact, Lieutenant, you did. And... oh yeah!... Guess what else happened.

Mr. Dooley: What?! What else happened, Barbara?

Barbara: Well, Lieutenant, while my mom was eating, she asked for you and I told her about what happened to Alofus. I told her that you were   checking up on him and your son, Little Jay, over at the M.A.V.A.S.H., but that you would be back over here to check on her as soon as you finished over there.

Mr. Dooley: Good; that was the correct thing to do, Barbara. Thank you, and I am on my way back to St. Mary's Hospital right now, so I'll see you and your mom shortly. Okay?

Barbara: Alright, Lieutenant, we will be looking for you, and I will let mom know that you are on your way over.

Mr. Dooley: Yeah, please do that for me, Barbara, and thanks.

**{Then Mr. Dooley hangs up the phone and heads to St Mary's Hospital.}

* [While en route, Mr. Dooley gets a phone call from his chief, Chief McClemens. Recognizing Chief McClemens' number, Mr. Dooley answers the phone...]*

Mr. Dooley: Hello?

Chief McClem: Okay; so you finally decided to answer my call, huh, Lieut. Dooley?

Mr. Dooley: Well, sir, it wasn't that I didn't want to answer your calls. It was just that I was seriously preoccupied with a couple of matters that warranted my undivided attention. It wasn't my intention to disobey your orders or disregard your authority.

Chief McClem: Oh really? And what, exactly, was so pressing that you felt you didn't have to take out a minute to call me in on it and receive my approval, Lieutenant?

Mr. Dooley: Sir, for one, when it comes to my family's safety, I personally don't feel like I have to answer to no one... As far as the situation surrounding Sgt. Willansby... well, sir, you already knew about that so I figured it wouldn't be prudent for me to be making calls at the time, for fear it might compromise Sergeant Willansby's ongoing investigation.

Chief McClem: Compromise?! How, exactly, would reporting to your chief compromise the investigation, Lieutenant Dooley? Will you please explain that to me, because I'm just dying to hear your answer.

Mr. Dooley: Chief McClemens, again, not to be disrespectful, sir, but right now, due to all that has happened... you know, with the circumstances involving Sergeant Willansby, things seem to have become very dangerous, even for us cops. So personally, I can't afford to trust anybody right now, sir, because the entire suspicion surrounding this matter is baffling... And that is the reason why I did what I did without informing you, sir.

Chief McClem: So what are you saying here, Lieutenant? To hell with policy?... Is that why you hung up on me?

Mr. Dooley: No, sir, I am not saying to hell with policy. What I am saying is that, when it comes to my family, if I have to sway a little bit from the rules, then I will do just that... And as far as hanging up on you, sir, I do apologize. I only did that because I had to attend to something immediately, and staying on the phone with you, trying to give you a step by step update, may well have jeopardized our successful rescue of Sergeant Willansby.

Chief McClem: I see... So again, what this all boils down to is you disobeying a direct order from you superior, Lieutenant. Well, this leaves me no choice but to file a report against you, Lieutenant Dooley, for insubordination... Now let's see how you and your family handle this one. *(Then the chief hangs up...)*

Mr. Dooley: Sir, why would you... Hello? Chief McClemens, are you there?... Hello?... Oh well; all's well, ends well.

**(Mr. Dooley makes that statement after realizing that Chief McClemens has hung up the phone on him, but he really doesn't care, because the energy of his attention is focused primarily on the recovery of Alofus and Serg. Willansby; so to concern himself with Chief McClemens' dogmatic threats is not at the top of his list.)

(Now arriving at St. Mary's Hospital, Mr. Dooley has parked his vehicle and is now on his way in. Upon entering, he is greeted by Barbara...)

Barbara: Well, hello there, Lieut. Dooley; good to see you.

Mr. Dooley: Hi, Barbara; good to see you too, sweetie. Is your mom awake or is she resting?

Barbara: She's awake. Ever since I told her that you were on your way, she has been asking me if you were here every five minutes.

Mr. Dooley: Well, let's not keep her waiting any longer; let's go on in to see her.

Barbara: Okay, but I must warn you, she's going to talk you to death.

[Mr. Dooley and Barbara are now at Serg. Willansby's door and Barbara is knocking...]

Barbara: Hello, mom, it's me and I have a surprise for you. Can we come in?

Serg. Willansby: Yeah, sweetheart. Please, come on in, ya'll; its okay.

(Barbara and Mr. Dooley enter Serg. Willansby's room. When Serg. Willansby sees Mr. Dooley, she immediately speaks out to him...)

Serg. Willansby: Hey there, Lieutenant. How are you doing, sir?

Mr. Dooley: I'm just fine, Sergeant Willansby. The real question here is, how are you, my dear?

Serg. Willansby: Well, considering everything that has transpired in the last couple of days, I guess I am doing pretty good.

Mr. Dooley: Yes, it does looks like you are doing pretty good, Sergeant, and I am happy to see that you are.

Barbara: Yeah, mom, God really did watch over you in this situation and I haven't stopped thanking him, because I'm not going to lie; at first, I was pretty pessimistic about them finding you, mom, but after talking to Lieutenant Dooley here, I was reassured that everything would be alright. For some strange reason, I had faith in what he was saying, and I believed him when he said everything would be alright and that they would find you.

Serg. Willansby: That's because Lieutenant Dooley has a way of convincing women to believe in him, sweetie.

Mr. Dooley: Now, Sergeant Willansby, let's not go there. Okay?

Barbara: What on earth are you guys talking about, mom?

Serg. Willansby: Well, honey, I think it's time for you to know the truth.

Mr. Dooley: Sergeant Willansby, please, this is not the place or the appropriate moment to bring up such a difficult and emotional conversation.

Barbara: Mom, what's going on here? What do you mean, it's time for me to know the truth?... Truth about what?

Mr. Dooley: It's nothing, honey. Your mom is probably under a lot of duress from her medication, right now, so don't pay her no mind. Okay?

Serg. Willansby: Duress?! I know you didn't go there, Lieutenant Dooley, or should I call you Jonathan? The only coercion was when you got me to keep quiet about *my...*

(Mr. Dooley interrupts Sergeant Willansby...)
Mr. Dooley: Sweet Pea, honey... please, for me and the sake of my family...

****{*All the while, Mr. Dooley is debating the issue of exposing whatever it is he doesn't want Barbara's mom, Serg. Willansby, to reveal. Barbara is in* *a state of awe and is curious about what's going on, but she remains quiet through it all.]*

Serg. Willansby: No, no way, Jonathan; not this time. It's not about your family anymore; I think it's time I thought about mine. Afterall, she is all I got... and I'm all she's got, Jonathan. This was a wake up call to me, as it should have been to you as well. I thought about it. If I had been killed, she would have never known, would she, Jonathan?... Answer me; would you have told her the truth even after she lost me, her mom, her only immediate family? Wouldn't that be fair? Doesn't she deserve to have what Diamerald and Little Jay have?

**{Serg. Willansby has been speaking to Mr. Dooley with tears in her eyes and anger in her voice for the last five minutes.}

*[By now Barbara, being a very bright young lady in her own rights, has picked up on what's possibly at hand. So now, as her mouth trembles, she begins to stammer ...)

Barbara: *Stop it!... Shut up!... Stop acting like I'm not standing here listening! [She turns and runs out of the room.]*

(Serg. Willansby calls for her daughter to come back, but to no avail. Barbara proceeds to run out of the door... Now Sergt Willansby turns to Mr. Dooley...)

Serg. Willansby: Well, aren't you going to go after her, or am I going to have to get up out of this hospital bed and go to our daughter's aid, Jonathan?

(Now a bit emotional himself, Mr. Dooley turns to Serg. Willansby...}

Mr. Dooley: Yes, I will go and see about our daughter, Sweet Pea... You stay there and rest, and I'll be back with Barbara. Okay?

**[Meanwhile, Barbara doesn't get too far down the hall anyway, because the officer posted outside Serg. Willansby's door chases her down and detains her. So of course, with Barbara being emotionally hysterical, she is down the hall, trying to fight off the officer, Officer Bradley...]*

Barbara: *Let me go!... Let me go!... I'm not under arrest; let me go!*

(Several onlookers stare at Mr. Dooley as he walks down the hall, toward Officer Bradley and Barbara... He has now made it to the two of them...)

Mr. Dooley: *(Talking to Officer Bradley) Stand down; I have everything under control from here... You may be excused.*

[Officer Bradley wanders back to his post outside Serg. Willansby's door. Mr. Dooley is now speaking to Barbara, while trying to hold her and pacify her...]

Barbara: *(screaming) Don't touch me!... Get away!... I don't want to hear it; leave me alone!*

Mr. Dooley: (rubbing Barbara's head and brushing her hair down) Barbara... Barbara... please hold on a minute, dear... please. I'm sorry, and perhaps I was wrong, sweetheart. I understand how you feel, darling, but please... at least hear me out. All I want is a chance to explain. Your mom needs you more than ever right now, Barbara, so please settle down and let's finally try to make this thing right. Okay, dear? Please, Barbara, just give me a moment.

[Barbara settles down a bit and appears to be adhering to Mr. Dooley's request... With Barbara in his arms, Mr. Dooley walks outside the hospital to talk to her. Considering all that has transpired, another one of his officers follows closely to watch his back; yet he gives them enough space and privacy to converse...]

{Now both of them are outside and Barbara is no longer acting hysterical over the sudden and newly discovered information, that Mr. Dooley is her *biological father. Mr. Dooley is now about to explain the circumstances surrounding this issue to her.}*

Mr. Dooley: (Looking Barbara square in her eyes) Okay, let's see here... Where should I begin?

Barbara: How about from the beginning, Jonathan, or should I say dad?... You know, like when you and my mom first decided to sleep together... and after doing so, I came along. How about you start there?

Mr. Dooley: Alright, Barbara, fair enough; then I will do that... Well, it was about twenty two years ago. Your mom and I were both trainees at the police academy. Seeing how beautiful your mom was, of course, I approached her and asked her out on a date after we all graduated.

Barbara: (Interrupting with sarcasm) Yeah, but of course, how can anyone resist such beauty? Even I fell in love with her irresistible charm.

Mr. Dooley: Barbara, please, stop it. It's not fair for you to be making a mockery of your mom's and my past affair, especially when you don't have all the facts yet.

Barbara: Fair?! Fair, Lieutenant?!... Oh, my God; its funny that you should talk about me being fair here when, for the past twenty one years, you denied your own child. So tell me... Go ahead. There's a real lesson here, isn't it?... And I can't wait to hear your doctrinaire, dad.

Mr. Dooley: Okay, Barbara, if you could just keep quiet long enough for me to explain all the facts surrounding this matter then, yeah, just maybe there is a lesson to be learned for all of us... But at least allow me to tell you what really happened so that you might better understand why your mom went along with this... because hating me is one thing, but I won't allow you to bash your mom, not for one second; she is one in a million.

Barbara: Oh, really? Then why isn't she Mrs. Dooley instead of Miss Willansby, Jonathan?

{Mr. Dooley is now angry...}

Mr. Dooley: (yelling) Alright, young lady, I've had enough back talking and disrespect for me and your mom! Now I am trying to, first off, tell you how sorry I am for not doing the right thing by letting everybody know the truth years ago... But it's not what you think here. What I was trying to tell you, Barbara, is that after the academy, your mom and I started dating, and everything seemed to be going well for about six months. But then, one evening, your mom came to me with this story about an ex boyfriend of hers. She said he was stalking her and that, for fear of us getting hurt, she had to call off the relationship. Well, of course, I was young, crazy, and in love with your mom. Plus I had recently graduated the police academy and was licensed to carry a gun. I told her that whoever that character was, we didn't have to be afraid of him, and that I wanted to meet him so I could put a stop to his threats. But your mom said no, and that she would take care of it herself. She also went on to tell me that she was carrying his child... Of course, that sparked an emotional fuse with me. We had a few words with each other and I stormed out of the house. We didn't speak to each other for almost three years, even though we were both on the force together. I asked my superiors for a transfer to another precinct, and I got it. During those three years, I never dated anyone else... until, one day, I was eating lunch at the Poe Pemp's restaurant. There was this young lady sitting across from me, all alone... Well, to be honest, she caught my eye, so I approached her and we talked briefly. Then we exchanged phone numbers... Well, Barbara, to make a long story short, today that young lady is Mrs. Dooley... Now as far as me being your dad, I didn't find that out until you were four years old.

What happened to your other dad, who also never made your mom his wife, is that... well, he found out that he had lung cancer and that he only had six months to live, so I guess, on his death bed, he decided to tell your mom something that he had been lying to her about for years, something that he now wanted to come clean with. That man, who your mom thought was your father, had gotten a vasectomy when he was twenty two years old, Barbara... and your mom met him when he was twenty four years old, so it was medically impossible for him to be your father. Now, of course, this made your mom and I rethink things in regards to the pregnancy, so we both agreed to take a DNA test, which came back 99.9% positive that you were my daughter, Barbara... And ever since that day, I have treated you that way, with the exception of publicizing it due to the fact that I had gotten married to Lillian and, prior to getting married, we had both respectfully acknowledged that neither of us had any kids... So for me to have come back into the marriage a year later and told her about you, that would have been a recipe for a suicidal divorce, especially when Lillian, herself, was seven months pregnant with our daughter, Diamerald, at that time... And that is why your mom and I mutually agreed not to bring this situation forward. Right now, this is all I can help you with, Barbara. Now the rest of this soap opera is left up to your mom to explain to you, although I would rather she volunteer it. I wouldn't advise you to pressure her under such conditions now; it might cause her to have an even more traumatic and emotional set back... And as for me, I concur with your mom about her abduction. She could have possibly lost her life through that ordeal. We need to go ahead and let Diamerald and Little Jay know that they have an older sister now, a very smart and beautiful one I might add. Barbara, if you can find it in your heart to forgive me, I would like for us to get a fresh start as father and daughter... And for what it's worth, honey, I love you. I always did, even before I found out that you were mine because you reminded me so much of the woman that I fell in love with over twenty two years ago. But she broke my heart... and that is where my wife, Lillian, came in at. She acted as a bandage for my heart, and that's why the last thing I wanted to do was to hurt her... But I am over all that stuff now. And though I still do love my wife, she will have to learn to love and accept you as my other child... Okay, now tell me, after hearing all the facts, how do you feel about me, Barbara?

Barbara: (while smiling) Wow! Honestly, Jonathan, I feel kind of sorry for you now, but I haven't exactly heard all the facts. I have yet to hear my mom's side of this story. So dad, for starters, I love you, too and I am glad to know that you are my father... And to have found out that I have two wonderful siblings like Little Jay and Diamerald warms my heart even more. So for now, let's just take this one day at a time. Okay? I don't know if we should even tell your family just yet, especially with all that's going on with my mom and Alofus right now... Anyhow, thanks for taking out the time to explain this to me. And I am sorry that it had to happen this way, but I am glad it did happen.

Mr. Dooley: Yeah, so am I, sweetheart. Now can we go back in and check on your mom?

Barbara: Of course, dad, let's do that. I'm sure she is probably worried sick.

Mr. Dooley: I see that you do know your mom, but if we don't hurry and get inside, she will be fighting the officer to get out here where we are.

Barbara: Yeah, I know, huh?... So I guess we best be heading back in.

**{So Barbara and Mr. Dooley, her dad, both head back inside of St. Mary's Hospital.}

**{They have gotten back inside and are entering Serg. Willansby's room. As they come in, Serg. Willansby sits up in her bed and looks at them, trying to see if she could possibly read their moods or demeanor, but to no avail.

Afraid that Barbara would have another emotional outburst if spoken to, Serg. Willansby decides to speak to Mr. Dooley...}

Serg. Willansby: Why, hello there, Lieutenant Dooley; good to have you all back... and thanks for going after Barbara for me.

Mr. Dooley: No thanks is necessary, Sergeant Willansby, it was the right thing to do. Besides, had I not gone after her, we would have had a half naked lady running down the hall, after her baby girl, with a drip attached to her arm.

*{Everyone laughs and then Serg. Willansby replies...}

Serg. Willansby: Now you got that right!

Barbara: Mom! You really would have ran behind me just as you are?

Serg. Willansby: Why, yes, I most certainly would have. I've done it before, when you were only five years old, baby girl... and I had on less than what I have on now.

Barbara: What?! When I was five?! What made you run behind me half naked when I was five, ma?

Serg. Willansby: Well, at five years old, you were just as curious as you are now, sweetie... We were at home, and I had just gotten into the shower to bathe. I left you in our living room, watching the television when all of a sudden, I felt a draft come underneath the bathroom door, which just so happened to be adjacent to the living room door that led to the outside... I heard the sound of a vehicle's tire screeching, so without hesitation or thought of wrapping a towel around me, I ran out of the bathroom to find that my thinking was on cue. You, little girl, had curiously wandered out of the front door, out into the street... And now there I was, running out to rescue my baby from getting ran over by a car. Fortunately, and thanks be to God almighty, the person in the vehicle was paying attention and was able to stop before hitting you, but unfortunately, now I was standing in the middle of the street, not half but entirely naked, with one hand covering where you came from and the other one reaching out to grab hold of you, Barbara.

Mr. Dooley: Wow! Are you serious, Sweet Pea? Did that really happen, or are you just trying to convince Barbara that you would have come after her?

Serg. Willansby: Now, come on Jonathan, would I lie about something like that?

Mr. Dooley: I'm not sure... Well, why did you keep it a secret from me all these years, and how did the public and your neighbors perceive you running outside nude?

Serg. Willansby: You know, Jonathan... and Barbara, my dear, please excuse mommy for this one... but frankly, at that point, I didn't give a damn about what anybody thought. Besides, I grabbed my baby, put her in my chest, and ran back inside as fast I could. I didn't come back out the door for about a month.

[Sergt Willansby starts laughing, and Barbara and Mr. Dooley joins in.]

Barbara: Mom, I would just like to say that if I really put you in such a precarious situation, I am so sorry... But next time, please, just take my wandering butt into the shower with you so you won't have to wander yours outside. Okay?

Mr. Dooley: Good idea, Barbara, I concur with you on that statement.

Serg. Willansby: You two may think it's funny... and I guess, when I look back on it, it's sort of funny to me, too... but it's a lot more emotional, because when I consider the reality of the matter, sweetheart, that could have possibly been our last day here on this earth.

Barbara: You mean my last day here on this earth, don't you, ma?

Serg. Willansby: No, I mean just what I said… because ain't no way I could have continued to live without you, sweetheart. You did then, as you do now, mean the world to me, Barbara… and nothing in the world could change this feeling that I have for you, baby.

Barbara: Alright, mom, you can stop now. I know that you love me, but that don't excuse why you chose not to tell me who my true father was.

**(The entire mood of everyone in the room changes. You can hear a pin drop. Barbara has taken off the face of glee and put on a face of sobriety. Mr. Dooley has dropped his head and taken a seat, and Serg. Willansby, who has yet to respond, also drops her head in shame. Barbara speaks further to her mom…)

Barbara: My God, mom… I mean, what were you thinking?… Obviously not about me or my feelings. Did you even, for one moment, consider my sensibility, mom?

(Mr. Dooley is not happy with the way Barbara is coming down on her mom, especially after all that she has gone through recently, with being kidnapped and all, so he speaks out to Barbara…)

Mr. Dooley: Now hold on here, Barbara, you have no right *to*… *[He is interrupted by Serg. Willansby.]*

Serg. Willansby: No, leave her alone, Jonathan. She is right and she does have rights. Even as infants, we all have rights… Remember what President Barack Obama said, in one of his campaign speeches, when they asked him the question about abortion?… You know, the one where they asked him when he thought an infant had rights, and he replied, "From the time of conception in the womb." So honey, you are well within your rights to question my judgment. I shouldn't have excluded you from my decision making, when it came to you having the right to know who your father was... And to be honest, there really weren't any excuses, only escape routes. We were both looking for ways to pacify our own selfish lives, not considering the most important thing that was at hand: you, Barbara, dear... a beautiful and sweet, little, innocent baby girl who didn't ask to born... You weren't planned, either but... through the excitement of, again, our own selfish, physical pleasures... you arrived. And now because of our... or, in this case, my mistake... I wanted to suppress your true identity.

Barbara: No, now you hold on, mom... Before you go any further, did you even know what my true identity was? Did you know who my father really was? Because in the defense of Lieutenant Dooley here... or Jonathan, whomever you want to call him... from my understanding, you kicked him to the curve, ma. You told him that you were impregnated by Raymond, who was your boyfriend at the time and also my alleged father... So I ask you, ma, did you know my true identity?

{Mr. Dooley looks on inquisitively, almost conformably, but with hesitation and reservation.}

Serg. Willansby: To be honest, sweetie, I thought I did. According to my calculation of the time that I had slept with Jonathan and the time that I had slept with Raymond... God rest his soul... well, you were supposed to have been Raymond's. Raymond had also lied to me for a couple of years. He had me to believe that he was fertile when, all along, he had gotten a vasectomy two years before I even met him. Anyhow, to make a long story short, Barbara... I confess, I blew it... I ran off a great and admirable young man who truly did love me, and he loves you, too, sweetie... very much. Ever since the day he found out that he was your father, he has not ceased with his financial responsibility of taking care of you, Barbara.

Barbara: Oh please, mama, give me a break! I am so tired of hearing about economics when it comes to loving a child. What about a child's first recital of a poem at school, or his or her first drawing that warrants both parents' approval, especially when they see that the other kids have both their parents present. Yeah, sure, I excused you because unfortunately, I thought that my dad was dead... But all the while, mom, you knew differently. Now was that fair to me, ma? Huh, was it?!

Serg. Willansby: No, sweetheart, it wasn't... But it also is not fair for you to stand here, twenty one years later, and judge me; to stand there and tell me that, if you were in my shoes, you would have done things differently when, honestly, you really don't know what you would have done, especially coupled with being in an emotionally and physically abusive relationship, in which baby girl, you don't think rationally... Trust me on this one. And as far as you dissing your father's financial support... well, look at it this way, you may not have gotten to go to college without it, dear. I mean, I'm just going to keep it real here. Of course you want your father to take you to the park, I'm sure most kids would, but if the ice cream truck happens to stop by the park and your loyal father, who wanted to spend time with his baby, doesn't have enough money in his pocket to get you that ice-cream bar, well, you and I both know that he is going to have problems, as would a father with his twenty one year old daughter when she grows up and finds herself working at a fast food restaurant because her parents couldn't afford college.

Barbara: But, mom, I had an academic scholarship.

Serg. Willansby: I know, fortunately for you... But what about those who don't, sweetheart?

Barbara: Okay, mom, I'm getting it. That's what I always hated about you; you were always able to manipulate your way out of our arguments. I wanted to continue on until I won or at least got my point over to you.

Serg. Willansby: Well, guess what honey... you won this one, sweetheart, because your point is well taken here; I assure you.

Barbara: For real? You mean it?

Serg. Willansby: Yeah, baby girl, I mean it. I'll never, ever get pregnant again and not tell the child, intentionally, who its father is.

Barbara: Mom, come on, don't beat up on yourself like that. After hearing both sides, I understand now. I just needed some closure for the emotional part, so that I could heal... But next time, if you don't mind, will you do one thing for me?

Serg. Willansby: What's that, sweetie?

Barbara: Will you at least allow nine months in between your sexual partners, so it won't be no questions as to who the father is?

**{Serg. Willansby and Barbara both laugh, but Mr. Dooley doesn't think that comment is funny at all. As a matter of fact, he tells them he has to go now.}

*{So Mr. Dooley hugs them goodbye and exits the room, leaving Barbara and her mom laughing and talking to each other.}

**{Meanwhile, back at the M.A.V.A.S.H., Alofus is about to come out of recovery, so Mr. Dooley calls Mrs. Dooley to inquire of the situation. The phone is ringing and Mrs. Dooley has just answered...}

Mrs. Dooley: Hello, sweetheart, I was wondering if you were gonna call or get back here in time to see Alofus come out of recovery.

Mr. Dooley: Now you know that I wouldn't miss an event as important as that is to Little Jay, honey. As a matter of fact, I am on my way there now. I'll see you all shortly. Okay?

Mrs. Dooley: Okay, dear, see you when you get here... Love you.

Mr. Dooley: Alright... Love you too, sweetheart.

(They both hang up. Mr. Dooley will be arriving at the M.A.V.A.S.H. in about fifteen minutes... He is now answering a call from Officer Bradley...)

Mr. Dooley: Hello, Lieutenant Dooley here.

Ofc. Bradley: Yes, Lieutenant Dooley, Officer Bradley here, sir... I am calling you in regards to the Satcher case.

Mr. Dooley: Yeah, okay, Officer Bradley. What about the Satcher case?

Ofc. Bradley: Well, sir, head quarters just contacted me because they could not reach you. I guess it was during the time you were collaborating with the young lady outside the hospital; I believe her name was Barbara. Anyhow a Dr. Chevonotsky, from the crime lab, said to tell you that they have possibly pulled a couple of prints, sir, and that you should get over there ASAP.

Mr. Dooley: Great! That's good news to me, Officer Bradley. Now here's what I want you to do: I want you to call this Dr. Chevonotsky guy back. Tell him I got his message, that I am on my way by there, and that I don't want him to give that info to anybody else, not even Chief McClemens. Is that understood, Officer Bradley?

Ofc. Bradley: Yes sir, perfectly understood. I'll get on it right away... Chief McClemens is not exactly my best friend either, sir.

Mr. Dooley: Alright, Officer Bradley. For the record, let's just keep those types of comments to our selves.

Ofc. Bradley: Okay, I'm sorry, sir... I got it.

**[Mr. Dooley hangs up and calls Mrs. Dooley again to inform her that, due to some sudden and very important business, he will be back at the M.A.V.A.S.H a little late. Of course, Mrs. Dooley isn't too happy about this, but she understands and says that she will convey this to Little Jay and Diamerald. And they say their goodbyes and hang up. So now, instead of heading to the M.A.V.A.S.H., Mr. Dooley is en route to J.P.D's crime lab to talk to Dr. Chivonotsky about the newly discovered evidence surrounding the Satcher case.]*

**{Meanwhile, back at the M.A.V.A.S.H, Alofus will be brought out of the recovery kennel and placed into the restorative kennel in about fifteen minutes, and Mrs. Dooley is about to tell Little Jay and Diamerald why their dad won't be there...}*

Mrs. Dooley: Diamerald... Little Jay... I just got off the phone with you all's dad... And he was calling to inform me that he had just gotten a call about some newly discovered evidence on a case that he was working; and that he regrets to inform us that he won't be joining us at the time Alofus will be coming out of recovery. However, he will be joining us a little later. So he asked me to apologize for him, and to let you all know that he was very sorry... But it could not be helped; for this meeting is very important.

Little Jay: More important than seeing Alofus, mom?

Mrs. Dooley: Well, son, I guess so. He also said, to this effect, that he believed that this investigation could probably help to solve the cases of Sergeant Willansby's kidnapping and Alofus' perpetrators. So you see there, Little Jay? Your dad is still out there, trying to find out who did this to Alofus. Aren't you proud of that?

Little Jay: Yeah, I sure am, mom. And I hope, when he does find them, that he locks them up forever and ever and throws away the keys, so that they won't be able to hurt Alofus or any other dog ever again.

Mrs. Dooley: And I am sure, son, that your dad will do just that.

Diamerald: Alright, mom, I heard all your speeches for dad, but he ain't getting off that easily with me. I'm not as naive as Little Jay. Just for once, dad needs to put our family before that police station.

Mrs. Dooley: Now Diamerald, your fa....

(*Wanting to straighten Diamerald, Kellie interrupts her sister, Mrs. Dooley...*)

Kellie: Diamerald, I'm not too fond of your dad, about certain things, either... And yes, he has missed a few family outings, on occasions. But one thing I am not going to do is stand by and watch you, for one, talk back to your mom, and two, misjudge your dad about him not putting you guys first. Now I've known Jonathan for just about as long as your mom. Ever since that night they met up at the Poe Pemp's restaurant, your mom and her kids... that's you two knuckle heads... have all been the apple of that man's eye. I know this is true because I remember when you, Diamerald, was in the hospital with a cyst of some sort on your leg and you had to be hospitalized for three weeks. That man, your dad, took off from that police station, and not one day passed that he wasn't there with your mom, Diamerald. Heck, I even missed coming to see you for a few days... and you never stopped loving your Auntie Kellie now, did you?

Diamerald: Why, no... no, ma'am... but I don't remember too much about that, Auntie Kellie.

Kellie: Yeah, that's it... I got you, Diamerald.

Diamerald: What, Auntie Kellie?

Kellie: I got you to admit, Diamerald, that you don't remember everything... and neither can your dad or any of us. We can't do everything every time; sometimes we will forget or just can't do it, baby girl... Now all I was trying to do was to get you to understand that we all love you: your mom, myself, Little Jay, Mark and Hanna here. Most of all, Diamerald, your dad loves you... more than you know. So before you go around bashing him, just take out a moment to think and to be thankful. Okay, sweetheart?

Diamerald: Yes ma'am, you're right, and mom, I am sorry for the way I carried on... not just for now, but for all the times I've talked too much.

Mrs. Dooley: Why, thanks for that apology, sweetie. I am so glad to see that my baby girl is finally growing up.

Little Jay: Yeah, me, too... because I've about had it with that big mouth of hers.

[Everyone laughs out loud.]

Diamerald: *(walks over to Little Jay and gives him a hug and a kiss on the forehead)* I love you, too, little boy. Now when are you going to grow up?

Mrs. Dooley: Okay, you two, we know that you both love each other. Sometimes I wish that your dad and I would have had one more child.

Little Jay & Diamerald: *(simultaneously)* Why mom?!

Mrs. Dooley: So that your big brother or big sister could act as a mediator between you two, and give me and your dad a break at times.

Diamerald: Okay, mom, so how is it that this quote, "other child" that you sometimes wish that you could have had would have been the first born? How come I couldn't have been the mediator person and let he or she and Little Jay fight each other?

Mrs. Dooley: I don't know, sweetheart, but you are right; you could have been the first one. Honestly, I don't know what possessed me to say that.

(Mrs. Dooley and her sister, Kellie, looks at each other with awe, wondering why she said that. It was a very mysterious coincidence, especially considering that neither of them knows that Barbara is Mr. Dooley's daughter, and she is older than Diamerald.)

**[As Mrs. Dooley stares at her sister, Kellie, Dr. Smortzen walks in along with Professor Greer. Dr. Smortzen is now speaking to the family in regards to Alofus' progression.}*

Dr. Smortzen: Why, hello there, Dooley family. Is everybody here? Are you all ready to see your dog, Alofus?

[As Little Jay jumps up and down, he and Mark screams, "Yeah, let's see him!"]

[Diamerald and Hanna are eager to see Alofus, too, but they prefer to be a bit more discreet than Little Jay and Mark...]

Diamerald & Hanna: Yes, Dr. Smortzen, we have been waiting patiently all day... Bring the stack of bones on out here.

(But then Diamerald sarcastically declares...)

Diamerald: Oh, my God, I forgot... he ain't bones anymore; he's a stack of rubber and wires now.

Mrs. Dooley: Now Diamerald, that's not nice. Look what you did to Little Jay's joy.

[Knowing that Diamerald might be right, Little Jay is now looking sad.]

Prof. Greer: Okay, now let's settle down here, everybody... Dr. Kyzar will bring Alofus out in a moment, but before he does that, there's something I would like to say to you all... I want to inform you all that you should not expect your dog to be as receptive to you as he was before. This is possibly due to the amnesia from the beatings he endured, coupled with some medication that we had to administer to him prior to his surgery. However, given time, he will come around slowly. His memory will gradually come back with numerous sessions of mental therapy. For instance, by you all coming around on a daily basis, this will be considered part of his mental therapy. And now, as for his physical state and appearance, it will look flawless. Everything went as planned and all the mechanisms seemed to be operating perfectly. In other words, the main surgery was a complete success... And with his routine therapy sessions and you all's fervent support, your dog, Alofus, will be up and back on track within 8 to 12 weeks... However, as we told you all earlier, he won't be ordinary but extraordinary; not normal but abnormal... Oh, I see Dr. Kyzar coming down the hall now, so everyone, please step out here in the middle of the room so that, when he rolls him in here, you will all have a full's eye view.

**(Dr. Kyzar has just come in. Alofus is laid out on a caged bed apparatus with various color coordinated wires and bandages. Little Jay,   Mrs. Dooley, Kellie, and Diamerald all have tears in their eyes. Little Jay walks over to Dr. Kyzar and asks him a question...)

Little Jay: Hey, doctor, what's with all the different types of color coded wires? And why ain't Alofus moving?

Dr. Kyzar: Well, Little Jay, all the multi-color wires are to let us know which is which. For instance, the curly, red wires are for muscle stimulation to the nerves in his back. The straight, blue ones are connections to the nerves in the brain. And the thick, yellow ones let us know if everything is operating correctly... The straight, red ones are to let us know if the spinal canal is still straight. See here, *(pointing to the small television monitor outside of Alofus' bed cage)* look at the screen. As you can see, all the different colored wires and labels showing up on the screen are to help us monitor Alofus' condition as it progresses or digresses. So this is it for now... From here on out, we just wait and see.

Kellie: And pray... If its okay with you and all the others, Dr. Kyzar, I would like for us all to join hands and send up a few words for Alofus.

Prof. Greer: Yeah, sure, ma'am. By all means, we encourage you all to do so.

(Everyone joins hands and bows their heads for prayer...)

Kellie: Father God in heaven, we come before the throne of grace, looking toward the hills from whence cometh our help... for we know that all of our help comes from you, Lord Jesus... asking that you will touch Alofus now, Father God. Touch him with your special touch. Show him your mercy. Dear Lord, help him to rise up and walk again, like he never walked before, to run like he never ran before, to see and hear like never before, Father God. We know that you can and are able to do this. Please, Jesus, let Alofus rise up for your cause, to be able to help other animals and humans alike to save them from bad, and evil men like the ones that attacked him. And lift him up, Lord Jesus, so the entire world will know that it's because of you, so that your name will be glorified. Thank you, Father God, now and forever more... Amen.

Dr. Smortzen: Young lady, I am glad that I was privileged to be a part of such a spiritual moment. And, believe it or not, the prayer that you were praying is basically the capacity in which Alofus will be serving.

Prof. Greer: Yes, he's right, you know. Alofus will be different and the world will look to him for more answers and research... And he could possibly be used as a tool to help fight crime like never before.

Dr. Kyzar: And not only that, for the record, we added a couple other extra features to your dog here. His head and chest are made of bulletproof materials. Yes, this animal here, when he gets back on his feet and one hundred percent mobile, will be a grave threat to the criminal world. We had that in mind when we were putting him back together, knowing that criminals were the ones that inflicted this debilitating state upon him in the first place.

Little Jay: So are you saying my dog, Alofus, will become sort of super hero dog?

Dr. Smortzen: Yes, that's exactly what we are saying, Little Jay. I'm sure Alofus will be well received, not only in this town, but throughout the world.

Prof. Greer: And just to pass along a little more information to you all, in regards to Alofus' popularity level, perhaps he will even be revered by people. I'm trying to paint a picture here, of the magnitude and affect that your dog will possibly have on the public's view of him. Well, I believe that Alofus will appear to be infallible, aspirational, or even perfect. But to be honest here, Mrs. Dooley, due to the foibles of Little Jay's youth, Alofus may initially have to be in an adult's custody, perhaps your husband.

Mrs. Dooley: What, exactly, does that mean, Professor Greer? I'm not quite understanding your language here.

Prof. Greer: What I am saying, Mrs. Dooley, is that, because of Little Jay's inexperience and his physical disability to control this animal, he is going to have to get prepared to pass the leash, so to speak. In other words, he won't be able to walk the dog anymore, at least for a while. You see,

Mrs. Dooley, we have a scarcity situation here, one that you can't just sashay your way into. This is a prerequisite of Alofus being released into the streets. Now don't misunderstand us here; we are ruful of the fact that Little Jay won't be able to get his dog back, as he initially thought, but given a particular time period, they will be able to reunite again. And mind you all, Alofus is no longer a single breed... well, at least from a technical perspective or term. Alofus is now legally termed a cur. For those of you who don't know what a cur is, it merely means that he is a dog of mixed breed now. But enough of all this scientific talk. Right now we have some unfinished business, so if you all will please excuse us... And I'm sure all of you are anxious to get back to your semi normal lives as well.

Dr. Smortzen: If I could just say one other thing before you leave, Little Jay... Try and look at it this way, at least Alofus is still with us. And as Prof. Greer said, just give it time. I promise you, before long, you and Alofus will be back in the frisbee business. Okay, son?

Little Jay: Okay, Dr. Smortzen, and thanks. Now does this mean we can go?

Dr. Kyzar: Yes, young man, if your mom is okay with that, this means you all are free to go home and finish sowing your oats.

Mrs. Dooley: You all won't get an argument out of me on that one. I can't wait to see what it's like to just sit and relax in my tub, at home, again.

Diamerald: Well, finally... Other than hearing that Alofus was okay, that's the best news I've heard today. Home sweet home.

Kellie: Diamerald, baby, Auntie Kellie concurs with you on that one.

(So on that note, everyone says goodbye and heads out the door to go home. However, the family is stll in danger, and the officers that Mr. Dooley posted has to see the family home and remain with them until Mr. Dooley says differently.)

(Meanwhile, Mr. Dooley has just arrived at the JPD crime lab to meet with Dr. Chivonotsky. He gets out of the car, walks inside, and is greeted by Dr. Chivonotsky...)

Dr. Chivon: Hello, how are you. sir?... Lieutenant Dooley I presume?

Mr. Dooley: Yes, that's me, and I see that you are Dr. Chivonotsky *(looking at his name badge)*. Nice to meet you.

Dr. Chivon: Likewise, Lieutenant Dooley. I've heard quite a bit about you.

Mr. Dooley: I hope that it won't interfere with you divulging your findings to me.

Dr. Chivon: *(laughs)* No, its not like that. They were actually good comments, Lieutenant. Anyhow, I don't want to waste your time discussing meaningless issues, so come with me and we will get on with the business that brought you here.

Mr. Dooley: Sounds good to me, Doc. Lead the way. *(They both enter into another room.)*

Dr. Chivon: Now, Lieutenant Dooley, the reason I asked you here concerns the case of the late Dr. Satcher. I think we have something, a very good something, I might add. There's a new technique being used in our C.S.I unit, and that is wave lengths of lights. These lights highlight patterns or impressions. If they could identify the source of the mark, this could possibly lead to our killer. What I am saying is that, if this new technique ends up finding a shoe imprint, then one of my associates will pull up a trace of a similar print from a web-site. If we get a match to the type of shoe from the imprint, then we might have a possible suspect or, as I said, even your killer, provided that we can determine the kind of shoe the suspect was wearing. We will run any and all the information through our police data-base. If this ends up being too big for us to handle, then we are prepared to bring in the FBI to help us with this investigation, something that I think you should be considering as well, Lieutenant Dooley. With the heinous nature of this crime, we consider the suspect, whomever he or she may be, to be a very dangerous individual, and we need to get them off the streets before someone else is hurt or killed. But for right now, we do not have any solid evidence as of yet, so until we can get a physical object to go with the imprint, even though we have a neighbor who is an eye witness to a suspect running away from the crime scene, we don't have much more to go on.

Mr. Dooley: Well, Dr. Chivonotsky, in regards to what you just shared with me, I am hopeful and convinced that we will get our guy. Let's just hope its not too late.

Dr. Chivon: I can tell you this, Lieutenant, if we get a match with the imprint and you get me a suspect and his shoe collection, we will get your killer.

Mr. Dooley: That's nice to know. However, right now, I gotta get out of here. My other half has been texting me for ten minutes now. So if you got one of them, then you know that we can't ignore those too long, or trouble is on the horizon.

Dr. Chivon: As a matter of fact, Lieutenant Dooley, I do have one of those and I can empathize with you... Now you go on and get out of here before she comes a knocking at my door.

{They both laugh and say goodbye. Mr. Dooley is now on his way home, to meet with his family. He is now dialing his wife, Ms. Dooley...}

The Author has Comprised a Group of Questions and Topics for Discussions. *Go ahead* Test your Reading and comprehensive Skills

1. When Dad *(Lieut. Dooley)* found out that Little Jay was being bullied, how did he feel? What steps did he take to remedy the problem?

2. When Diamerald decided to leave home to go off to college at what age was this? What was the name of her roommate?

3. In the end Barbara finds out who her real father is, who is it? Is she happy with the final analysis?

4. One of Lieut. Dooley's officers openly admitted that he didn't like Chief McClemens-Who was this?

5. Chief McClemens had two half brothers who were they? What happen to one of them?

6. Ms. Dooley and Lieut. Dooley met each other prior to getting engaged. Where did they first become acquainted?

7. Sgt. Willansby had a boyfriend who had abused her in the past--What was his name? What lie did he tell her that had a major impact on her and Lieut. Dooley?

8. Ms. Dooley said to her daughter Diamerald that she was glad to see that she was growing up. What did Diamerald do to cause this statement?

9. There were three main characters responsible for Alofus successful surgery--Who were they?

10. The DVM said Alofus would be ready to go within how many weeks?

An Excerpt from the Coming Vol. 2 of this First Edition of

"Man's Best Friend"

In volume 2 of the first edition of "Man's Bestfriend" Lieut. Dooley and Alofus are about to become crime fighting partners. This will prove to be a good combination of a dynamic duo crime fighting team. Because Lieut. Dooley is soon to find out that Money Mike *(aka)* Alfred Kincade is a bionic man--a human version, if you will of what Alofus has become. So Lieut. Dooley will need someone or something to help aid him in the apprehension of Money Mike and a host of other villains, which are to be exposed also in Vol. 2. To find out the conclusion of this matter, stay tuned and look for Vol. 2 of the first Edition of "Man's Bestfriend." Coming soon to your favorite Bookstores.

By John A. Greer Sr.

CONTENTS

Part IV.

Meanwhile back at the Police Station

1. Finding out more about Money Mike through Sergeant Williansby
2. Meeting with Professor Greer.
3. Who I'm more afraid of it's certainly not the police.

Part V.

"Man Best Friend" Vol. 1 (closing]

This is not the end, but the beginning of many things to come from this new Author John A. Greer Sr. who would like to thank you all for taking out your precious time to read along with him in his first edition of vol. 1 "Man's Best Friend" and he ask that you all stay tuned for vol. 2 of the first edition coming soon to a book store near you. And In closing He would like to leave these proverbs with you the readers... To Always Remember.]

"When choosing a book to read"

     Choose one that you can understand, one the carries the D-scarf syndrome.

"A great patriot once said... In all they getting--get an understanding"

     And that's exactly what one would be getting when reading books with the D-scarf-syndrome in mind.

                             By John A. Greer Sr.